THREADING THE NEEDLE

THREADING THE NEEDLE

The PAX NET Story

LOWELL "BUD" PAXSON

WITH GARY TEMPLETON

HarperBusiness
A Division of HarperCollinsPublishers

HarperCollins books may be purchased for educational, business, or sales promotional use. For information please write: Special Markets Department, HarperCollins Publishers, Inc., 10 East 53rd Street, New York, NY 10022.

FIRST EDITION

Designed by Nancy Singer Olaguera

Library of Congress Cataloging-in-Publication Data

Paxson, Lowell
    Threading the needle : the PAX NET story / Lowell "Bud" Paxson. — 1st ed.
        p. cm.
    ISBN 0-88730-948-8
    1. Paxson, Lowell. 2. PAX NET. 3. Television broadcasting—United States. I. Title.
HE8700.8.P39   1998
384.55'523—dc21   98-19272

98 99 00 01 ❖/RRD 10 9 8 7 6 5 4 3 2 1

I would like to dedicate this book to . . .
My wonderful wife and best friend, Marla, truly a gift from God,
who has made my life happier than I ever could have hoped for . . .

My children, their spouses, and my grandchildren, for whom my love has never faltered, although, as an entrepreneur,
I have not spent nearly enough time with them, as a father or as a family.
I am grateful for their love and patience and may they always know how much I love them and need them . . .

My Lord, Jesus Christ, whose love for me I cannot fathom;
to whom I owe all that I have, all that I am, and all that I ever will be.

CONTENTS

It is easier for a camel to go through the eye of a needle than for a rich man to enter the kingdom of God.

Luke 18:25
New International Version

1

THE NEEDLE'S EYE

"Ladies and gentlemen, I'm holding a box in my hands. It's a beautiful, colorfully printed box containing an electric Rival can opener. The price is printed right on the side of the box, $14.95."

I then read the selling points printed on the side of the box. "Fits on any kitchen counter. Opens any can. It's light. It's electric (UL approved). It's modern.

"I'll sell these for $9.75, and if you'd like to have one, then call the radio station and we'll take your name and phone number. But you have to come to the station and pick it up before twelve noon. You also have to come with a check or cash, because we don't take credit cards. If you want one, call the station."

A moment after I made the announcement, all five phone lines at the station lit up. The receptionist, the announcer, and I went from one line to another taking orders.

That afternoon I deposited $800 in the bank and made payroll for my AM radio station. As I sat in the bank reflecting on what had happened that morning, a dream unfolded in my mind. I knew in that moment that I had stumbled across something that would provide the world with a whole new way of buying and selling products. I also realized I was never going to sell advertising on AM radio again, and I was into the business of selling products.

It started in 1977 when I owned an AM radio station on the west coast of Florida. I had only had the station for a short time when I learned about a lawyer, Roy Speer, who had a license to build an FM station in a nearby market. The two of us met at his office, and I told him I wanted to buy his FCC construction permit for the FM station.

He smiled and said, "You can have it for $100,000."

I looked across the desk and responded, "Mr. Speer, you can only sell a construction permit for what you've invested in it. Not a nickel more." The Federal Communications Commission's (FCC) rules prevent making a profit on an unbuilt station.

"That's un-American!" Roy responded.

"Yea," I said, "but that's the way it is. That's the law."

The discussion might have ended there, but it didn't. Instead, Roy checked my background and figured out that together we would have a very successful FM station. He said he'd put up the money and I could run it. We'd own it fifty-fifty. We sealed the deal, and in 1978 the FM station was on the air and our partnership was up and running.

CAN OPENERS FOR CASH

While we owned the FM station together, I remained the sole owner of the AM station. At the time, in the late seventies, while FM radio's popularity was growing, AM's audience was declining, causing many of my AM advertisers to be slack about paying their bills. One Thursday afternoon, I needed some cash to make Friday's AM payroll. When no checks arrived in the mail, I climbed in my van and made personal visits to some of our delinquent accounts. One was a high-volume appliance dealer, who had the largest showroom in the area.

When you entered his store, you couldn't miss the guy's office. It was right in the middle of the sales floor, a square room with glass walls on all four sides. It looked like an aquarium. He liked the glass walls because he was able to monitor what was happening in the store. Unfortunately, it also enabled customers to see in his office. He had papers scattered all over the room. There were advertisements stacked on his desk and invoices piled high on file cabinets. My check could have been hidden in that mess and never been found.

I walked up to the glass door of his office and knocked. He waved me in, and I opened the door and stuck my head inside.

"You're the thirteenth radio salesman who has come by here today," he barked at me. "If you're here to try to sell me radio advertising, then don't bother coming in. But if you'd like to join me for a drink, come on in."

Well, I wasn't there to sell him anything, so I walked in. He motioned to a padded chair.

As we sat there making small talk, I said, "I'm not here to sell you anything."

"That's good," he replied. "Because if you were, I'd take away your drink and throw you out the door."

"I'm here to collect the money you owe me."

"What do you mean *collect*?" he asked.

"You owe me $1,000 and I'm here to collect it."

"You're out of your mind. I don't owe you a nickel," he shouted.

I reached in my pocket and pulled out a folded invoice. "Here's the bill," I said as I handed it to him.

"Well, that advertising didn't work and I'm not going to pay you," he insisted.

At about that time I could see something click in his mind. He turned to me with a smile and said, "However, I'm overstocked with electric can openers. I have 112 I'd like to get rid of. You can take them as payment in full."

He was pretty excited about the idea. He probably had

paid a wholesale price of $500 or so for all the can openers, but he would give them to me at their retail price of $1,000. To make things even better, he had some sort of an arrangement in which he could submit a paid advertising bill and collect a $500 advertising rebate from the manufacturer. What a deal! He took a slow-moving product off his shelves, put $500 into his account, and paid for his advertising. He did all of that and it didn't cost him a dime.

What choice did I have? I could take the can openers or I could take nothing. So I took the can openers.

The two of us loaded them into my van, and I drove back to the station. Because it was a daytime station and went off the air at 5:00 P.M., nobody was there when I returned. Under the cover of darkness, I hauled the can openers from my van into the hallway. I went home without a clue as to what I would do with all of those can openers. The next morning I woke up realizing that I still did not have the money for payroll. I had no choice but to take $800 out of my savings account, and my savings passbook was at the office. Frustrated, I stomped out to the van, climbed in, started the engine, and drove to the radio station.

Shortly after 9:00 A.M., I walked into the station and saw the can openers stacked in the hall. At the same time I heard our morning radio personality for our call-in talk show speaking over the air with someone on the telephone.

In that moment a thought entered my mind that would change my life forever. I acted on it.

I opened the door to the studio and told the host, "You've got a guest on your show this morning." Unaware of what was going on, he stammered into the microphone, "All right, we have a guest this morning."

He handed me the mike and continued, "You're the owner of the station, so you can do or say anything you like."

I took the microphone and began, "LADIES AND GEN-
TLEMEN . . . "

Fifteen minutes later, all 112 can openers had been sold,
and by noon 85 had been picked up.

From that day until 1983, I sold all sorts of merchandise
over the AM radio station: hair dryers, gift certificates, jewelry, makeup, electronics, and just about anything else you can
imagine. The only market research we ever did was to offer
something on the air, and if it didn't sell we never offered it
again.

By 1982, Roy and I agreed to sell the radio stations. We
sold the FM for $900,000 and I sold the AM for about
$300,000.

"What are you going to do with your profit?" Roy asked.

"I want to continue selling merchandise, but I want to sell
it on TV over cable television."

"How much money will you need to get started?"

"Around $500,000."

Roy offered to put up all the money so I could keep my
profit and begin to build up my net worth. I accepted. We
agreed on a sixty-forty split. Roy would own 60 percent and I
would own 40 percent. Thus was launched the Home Shopping Network.

When we first introduced the idea to the public, marketing
experts predicted our venture was doomed to fail. "Nobody
will buy something from just seeing it on television," they
said. "The idea is ludicrous," they insisted.

Were the critics ever wrong! The first year we did $12 mil-
lion in business. The next year sales soared to $24 million,
and in 1985 we leaped to $50 million. In May 1986, we went
public with a record opening on Wall Street, and we finished
1986 at $160 million. Sales continued to rise to $560 million,
$780 million, and finally, in 1990, passed $1 billion.

AN ANONYMOUS HELPER

How did we do it? I could tell you we were skilled entrepreneurs who were looking for just such an opportunity, but the truth is we were just plain lucky. I know we didn't go and find success. It found us. Actually, I prefer to think that Tess in the CBS hit *Touched by an Angel* was right when she said, "Luck is when God wishes to remain anonymous."

I must admit that once the idea of using TV to sell merchandise captured our imaginations, we knew how to run with it. As we ran we had the privilege of changing the way many Americans shop.

PAPER ROUTE OR HAMSTER

My success with the Home Shopping Network, infomercials, radio stations, and now the formation of a new television network, PAX NET, began when I was very young.

I remember as a kid asking my dad for $5. Instead of giving me the money, he told me to go and get a paper route. That sounded like a good idea, but before rushing down to the local newspaper I decided to talk with a friend who already worked for the newspaper.

"What do you do for your paper route?"

He was really excited at the opportunity to tell me about his job. "Well, I get up at five-thirty in the morning, then I go get the papers, fold them, and stuff them in a bag. Once I've done that, I put the bag on my bike and ride a trail that I've been given by the paper. I then throw the papers on the front porches of the houses on my route."

"You do that every day?" I queried.

"Yes, and on Sunday I have to get up at four-thirty in the morning 'cause the paper's twice as thick. Since the paper is heavier, I deliver half of them and then go back to my house to get the rest. Oh, I also have to collect the money one evening a week."

"You do all that and make $5 a week?" I asked.

"That's right!" he said with a smile.

I remember thinking to myself, *There's got to be a better way!* It was at that moment that I decided I'd rather work for myself.

After some checking around, I learned that a company in town would buy all the adult hamsters I could supply for $1 each. In a short time, I had several cages and enough female hamsters to provide the company with twenty hamsters a week. All I had to do was run downstairs in the morning, feed the hamsters, give them water, and clean their cages once a week. It was a lot less work than a paper route, more fun, and four times the money.

That experience was formative for me, because it proved I could make more money working for myself than for someone else.

I've always thought it fascinating that my buddy who threw the papers was left-handed and I'm right-handed. The first business to the left of his home was a funeral home, where he got his first job, and he has ended up owning some of the largest funeral homes in the area. The first business to the right of my house was a radio station, where I got my first job, and I've been in broadcasting ever since.

Sometimes being in the right place seems as simple as stepping outside your front door and turning in the direction that comes naturally. Of course, there is a lot more to building a business than being in the right place at the right time. And there's more to it than good luck.

Over the years, I've learned that *true* success is more than simply making money. It involves more than increasing the profit margin of your company so you can exercise greater influence and live more comfortably.

While I don't mean to diminish the importance of financial profit, I have come to realize the need to strive for both purpose and balance. Through much of my life, I strove for success and money and paid little heed to family relationships or to God.

THE NEEDLE'S EYE

The challenge of living a balanced life isn't new. In the late 1980s, as I was gaining wealth, a personal crisis forced me to seek God. In that time of despair, I was greatly influenced by the story of the rich young man who approached Jesus and asked how he could acquire eternal life. Jesus told him to obey God. The young man said he had done that since he was a kid. In order to let the man prove his commitment to God, Jesus told him to sell his possessions, give the money to the poor, and follow him. The man didn't expect that! Because he had a lot of money, he gave up his quest.

Jesus told the man, "It is easier for a camel to go through the eye of a needle, than for a rich man to enter the kingdom of God" (Luke 18:25). Those words shocked the crowd of curious onlookers because they believed financial prosperity proved God loved a man. If a wealthy man couldn't enter God's kingdom, with all his money, they wondered who could.

Jesus said, "What is impossible with man is possible with God" (Luke 18:27).

Those words have had a profound effect on my life, as well. As a Christian, I recognize that salvation is a gift from God that cannot be earned, but I am very much aware of the tension between depending on God and being self-reliant.

That is why I like the graphic image Jesus used. On one hand, it reminds me that I need God in my life. I cannot get to heaven on my own.

The other half of the image focuses on the needle. I like to think of threading the needle as passing God's muster; it is not that I have to earn my salvation, but I want to bring all my ideas, my plans, and my resources before him to be sure I'm operating within his will and not solely on my own. It's like one of those sample boxes at an airport that says, "If your bag won't fit in here, it won't fit on the plane."

While the passageway is narrow, the good news is that God's grace can enable even a camel to get through. That has given me hope. It has helped me concentrate on God and not the money. It also gives me reason to try to figure out how I can cooperate with God in my business and in my family's life.

As I reflected on the imagery of the needle, it occurred to me that each of us has three threads, or elements, of life we need to get through the needle's eye: the business or career thread, the spiritual thread, and the family thread. Our responsibility is to cling to the grace of God while we seek to maintain the purpose and balance our lives need so we can thread the needle. "The love of money is a root of all kinds of evil," and many who fixate on their wealth never get through God's needle.

In an impersonal, high-tech society, it's easy for us to forget that we have been created for a higher purpose. We can lose sight of the fact that our lives can make a difference and the money we amass can be used by God for His purpose. After all, it's all His.

I like to tell the story of the American Indian who found an eagle's egg and put it into the nest of a prairie chicken. The eaglet hatched with the brood of chicks and grew up with them. All his life, the eagle, thinking he was a prairie chicken, did what the prairie chick did. He scratched in the dirt for seeds and insects to eat. He clucked and crackled. He flew in a brief thrashing of wings and flurry of feathers no more than a few feet off the ground. After all, that's how prairie chickens were supposed to fly.

Years passed and the eagle grew up. One day, he saw a magnificent bird far above him in the cloudless sky. Hanging with graceful majesty on the powerful wind currents, it soared with scarcely a beat of its strong golden wings.

"What a beautiful bird!" said the eagle to a friend. "What is it?"

"That's an eagle, the greatest of the birds," the neighbor clucked, "but don't give it a second thought. You could never be like him." Therefore, the eagle never gave it another thought, and he died thinking he was a prairie chicken.

What a tragedy. That bird was created to soar into the heavens, but he was conditioned to stay earthbound. Though designed to be among the most awesome of all birds, he instead believed his neighbor's counsel.

We're all designed to accomplish a purpose far greater than we can imagine. God has a plan for our life. We're not here simply to grow up, gain an education, get married, find a job, make money, have children, grow old, and die. We must resist the tendency to view our lives in that way. Instead, we need to tap into the grace of God so we can pursue the highest level of life. God intends for us to soar like the eagle.

A LIFE OF BALANCE

To accomplish our purpose requires making up our minds that we will diligently seek to bring balance to the three crucial threads of our life (the business thread, the spiritual thread, and the family-values thread). Balance requires two things. First, we must trust God to do the work that only he can do, but we must accept our responsibility to use all of our resources and abilities to accomplish the task at hand. I recently heard a story that illustrates the point.

A man once made an investment in a large farm that he hoped to enjoy during his years of retirement. While he was still holding down a full-time job, he would take every Saturday and go out to his land and work. What a job it turned out to be! He soon realized he had bought acres of weeds, gopher holes, and rundown buildings. It was anything but attractive. Yet the man knew it had potential and he stuck with it.

Every week he would go to his farm, crank up his small tractor, and plow through the weeds with a vengeance. Then he would spend time doing repairs on the buildings. He'd mix cement, cut lumber, replace broken windows, and work on the plumbing. It was hard work, but after several months the place began to take shape. Every time the man put his hand to some task, he would experience a deep sense of gratification. He knew his hard work was paying off.

When the project was completed, the man received a neighborly visit from a farmer who lived a few miles down the road. Farmer Smith took a long look at his neighbor and cast a longer eye over the revitalized property. Then he nodded his approval and said, "Well, sir, it looks like you and God really did some work here."

Wiping the sweat from his brow, the man answered, "It's interesting you should say that, Mr. Smith. But I've got to tell you—you should have seen this place when God had it all to himself!"

The story illustrates the importance God places on partnership. Without God doing his part, there would have been no farm at all. When the farmer fulfilled his part of the responsibility, the farm became beautiful and productive. Daily, God calls us into partnership with him.

It takes hard work to achieve a higher purpose in life. There is no shortcut that makes a life of balance easy. Yet God offers us his love and grace as we diligently try to thread the needle. As we try to do our part, God guarantees He will do His.

The purpose of this book is to help you know how you can do your part—how you can work with God in your business to serve Him in some way, then watch God grow your business so you can serve Him more. I certainly don't want to give the impression I've somehow arrived. I haven't, as those who know me are quick to point out. A lot of people are watching to see if I can get my camel through the eye of God's needle. But I have discovered some principles that have given me confidence as I pursue the greatest opportunity of my life—the development of PAX NET—a television network aimed at providing viewers with family-values-oriented programming. In the next chapter you'll find out where this dream came from and how you can nurture and develop your own dreams with God's help.

2
BELIEVE THE DREAM

Never in my life had so much rested on a decision someone else would make, a decision over which I had no control.

By March 31, 1997, Paxson Communications had purchased forty-seven radio stations and sixty television stations, many in major markets in the United States. Never in television history had one company bought so many TV stations so quickly. Those familiar with the situation knew the future of Paxson Communications' TV stations depended on an impending Supreme Court decision. In a case known as "Must Carry," the High Court would decide whether or not cable systems *must carry* the programming of local TV stations. Those nine judges held the future of Paxson Communications in their hands. A ruling supporting the "Must Carry" law would mean our stations could piggyback their signals on the systems of the nation's largest cable companies and have access to homes hooked up to those cable systems. A negative ruling would mean our stations would only be viewed by those television sets not connected to a cable system. This would limit our viewing audience to those with televisions that could pick up our signal with an outside antenna or rabbit ears. Of course, the cable operators had brought the lawsuit against "Must Carry" because they didn't want to have to carry all of the local stations.

Since the popular opinion was that the Supreme Court would overturn "Must Carry," many Wall Street pundits believed I had led Paxson Communications down the proverbial plank and was about to step over the edge, plunging the company into financial ruin. Paxson Communications' public stock (AMEX-PAX) slid downward. As the day of the final decision rolled around, I posted a colleague outside the doors of the Supreme Court with a cell phone. When the ruling came, I wanted to be the first to know. A favorable ruling would tell me the dream and feeling that I had believed came from God would soon become a reality.

THE IMPORTANCE OF DREAMING

Nothing is more important to the development of a business career, or any endeavor, than the dream it's seeking to fulfill. Effective leaders are visionaries. They see something out there in the distance that others don't yet see. They're convinced that the ordinary can be transformed into something successful. Leaders have a vivid imagination, and they're persuaded that what is only a distant dream today will be a reality tomorrow.

I'm probably safe in saying that almost every major scientific and social breakthrough in human history flowed from a visionary. A few years ago, the magazine *Esquire* devoted an entire issue to "50 Who Had Made the Difference." Lee Eisenberg, contributing editor, wrote in his introduction to the section on nine visionaries: "While their contemporaries groped at the present to feel a pulse, or considered the past to discern the course that led to the moment, these nine squinted through the veil of the future. Not that they were mystics . . . For most of them, reality was pure and simple. What set them apart was the conviction that a greater reality lay a number of years down the pike" (Lee Eisenberg, "Taking the Long, Sharp View," *Esquire,* 1983, 100 [6], 305).

Vision is seeing what others don't see. And when those with a shared vision from God come together with God, something extraordinary occurs.

FROM POLECAT CREEK TO THE ANNALS OF HISTORY

No one in Polecat Creek, North Carolina, thought Egbert Roscoe would amount to much. Why should they? His home certainly didn't provide him with the kind of support often associated with the development of greatness. His father, a big man, seldom uttered a word. His mother, while overcome with nervousness much of the time, made all of the family decisions. She was so religiously paranoid that she reportedly refused to say "Hello" when answering the telephone, because, as she would whisper to friends, "That word contains the name of Satan's home." Instead, she would pick up the phone and say, "Hey-Yo."

Egbert's hometown didn't provide the growing boy with much intellectual or cultural stimulation either. His father had failed as a farmer, and when Egbert was five the family moved to Blanchard, Washington, where he grew up in a logging camp.

Surrounded by the sound of saws cutting through tree trunks and giant firs crashing to the ground, Egbert could have tried to figure out how he could support himself as a logger. But Egbert nursed a different dream, a dream others might have scorned. In spite of his circumstances or background, Egbert refused to limit his dream. He knew that one day he would address millions.

In 1926 Egbert graduated from Washington State College, a school noted for its speech department and one of the first to offer courses in radio broadcasting. Egbert's voice became his greatest asset. But he possessed more than a rich voice. He had gained a reputation as a debater and sports broadcaster.

Tired of the endless jokes about his name, in 1928 he changed Egbert to Edward and shortened Roscoe to a middle initial. Edward R. Murrow went on to become one of the greatest broadcasters in radio and television history. Unlike any other commentators on the air before 1941, Murrow understood the difference between broadcasting and the printed word. Some called him the musician of the spoken word.

In my office hangs an autographed picture of Edward R. Murrow. It serves as a reminder of someone who believed in his dream and pursued it. Many people remain victims of their circumstances. Visionary leaders see what others cannot see and go after it with unbridled enthusiasm.

CUP SALESMAN TO BILLION-DOLLAR BUSINESS

Ray Kroc, of McDonald's, is another classic example of an individual who never gave up on his dream. He had spent seventeen years of his life as a salesman for the Lily Tulip Cup Company when he decided to venture out into the milkshake-machine business. A machine that could mix a number of shakes at the same time fascinated him.

He had heard that the McDonald brothers in San Bernardino, California, were turning out forty milk shakes at one time on eight of his six-spindled multi-mixer machines. Upon investigation, he was impressed with their assembly-line approach to milk shakes, burgers, and fries. He asked the McDonald brothers, "Why don't you open other restaurants like this?"

They objected, saying, "It would be a lot of trouble and we don't know anyone who could get them open." In that moment, Ray Kroc had a vision begging for implementation. Though he was old enough to think about retirement, he was able to build his new hamburger chain into a billion-dollar business in just twenty-two years. He saw what others could not see, and it paid off with a pair of golden arches that are recognized around the world. Kroc and Murrow saw what others hadn't seen. They both imagined something that went beyond the ordinary, beyond what others thought possible.

BECOMING A VISIONARY LEADER

Frankly, I've always been a dreamer. I always knew how to see opportunity where others saw little. But most of the dreams I tried to bring into reality evaporated before anything came of them. (I'll tell you more about that later.) Fortunately, experience—which comes with repeated failure—helped me sharpen my entrepreneurial skills. That, along with the development of my spiritual life, helped me learn how to see and articulate dreams through God's eyes, which ones to pursue and how to bring them into reality. Threading the needle involves skillfully growing and bringing those dreams into reality by God's grace. In the remainder of this chapter, I'll share with you the first step that must be taken in the development of a dream, and in the next chapter I'll give you three additional steps.

Step One: Grow the Dream

I'm not sure exactly how Edward R. Murrow and Ray Kroc cultivated their dreams. But I suspect neither of them began with a clear vision of precisely what they would do and how it would be done. The visionary leaders I've had the privilege of knowing possess a unique ability to grow dreams. Growing a dream is vital, but I've learned to grow a dream with God's help. Without it I know I would fail.

BIRTH OF THE DREAM

In early 1991, I sold my interest in the Home Shopping Network (HSN) and Silver King Communications—twelve television stations I had purchased or built for the company—and walked away with $130 million in my pocket. At the time I wasn't sure what business venture I'd pursue next. My friends urged me to bank my chips and retire.

I actually followed their advice. I went to the beach. It was a great day. But after a single day off I realized I needed to work. Seriously, one day out of the game of commerce was all I could handle. I felt like an athlete sitting on the sidelines watching everyone else play. I love the game and had to get back on the field.

Even before I had left HSN God had been developing a dream in my mind. I wanted to create a twenty-four-hour television program that would be different from anything else on the air. It would offer people hope by reminding them of God's love and presence. I didn't want the program to be a platform for preachers or to be a conduit to collect the viewer's money. I felt there was already too much of that on the air. Instead, it would offer people hope by reminding them of God's presence and his love.

Once God's dream captured me, I read every book I could find on the topic of worship, and within three weeks I had written a complete nonprofit business plan. The details of God's dream flowed from me like water from a pitcher.

By September 1992, our small team had spent millions of dollars building TV facilities, assembling staff, and creating the programs. We developed videos, combining the most exquisite scenes from nature with beautiful Christian music, and overlaid the scenes with scripture. The product was everything I had dreamed it would be. We gave it a simple name: The Worship Network.

I intended to make *Worship* available to every Christian station in the country, but nobody wanted it unless we paid for the time. We had determined we were not going to ask for money from our viewers. We weren't there for that purpose. We didn't want to take from them—we wanted to give to them.

Without a viable alternative, we bought time on Christian stations to get *Worship* on the air. Immediately, we had a problem. We were sandwiched between the so-called faith healers and the prosperity preachers. In the programs that preceded ours, viewers were told if they believed and sent money they would be healed. After our program they were told if they would believe and send in a contribution they would get rich. Our target audience—the people who needed to be reminded of God's love—weren't watching those programs. They avoided them. We had the right product but we were on the wrong street corner.

Twenty-four months later, after losing between one and two million dollars a year, we pulled *Worship* from the Christian stations and began transmitting from a satellite twenty-four hours a day into about three million homes equipped with satellite dishes. What's amazing is that without being asked for a dime the viewers showed their support by sending in contributions. They clearly liked the network, but we had a problem—expenses were far exceeding income. It didn't take rocket scientists to realize we needed a more afford-able way to deliver the product.

At the same time we were creating *Worship*, my friend Jim Bocock, from Home Shopping, and I began buying radio stations, forming Paxson Communications Corporation, and had taken the company public. Because we were doing so well with our radio stations, we decided to buy a television station. In December 1993 we closed the deal on our first television station, in Miami, and put on *Worship* from 11:00 P.M. until 7:00 A.M. The rest of the time, we decided to air infomercials. That was a stroke of luck! (Again, God's anonymous help.) I called everybody I knew from my years at the Home Shopping Network who was creating infomercials and sold time on the station. By the middle of January we were making money and reminding people of God's love and presence in their lives.

Letters poured in from all over Miami. People from every race and religion wrote letters telling us how the late-night show *Worship* was touching their lives.

Little did I know at that time that the experience would give birth to a much bigger dream. *Worship* would eventually give life to a network of stations that would remind people of God's love through family-oriented programs like *Touched by an Angel*.

THE DAY THE BEEPERS WENT SILENT

Over the next few years I watched (sometimes in amazement) as God guided our dream. I was always fascinated with little affirmations along the way. Some would call them "coincidental," but I saw them as God's way of saying, "We're in this together."

On May 19, 1998, like everyone else in America, I listened to the reports that a satellite carrying the signal for most of the pagers in the country had fallen out of the sky, sending doctors and hospitals (as well as everyone else in the country) into a panic. At first, I didn't realize the significance it carried for Pax Net, but before the day was over I was aware that God had answered my prayer by giving me a needed affirmation and, moreover, protected us from a real disaster.

The story began back in 1991 when we were looking for a way to get the Worship Channel into American homes. We contracted with Pan Am Sat to lease a transponder on the satellite Galaxy 6. This allowed *Worship* to deliver its signal to our individual stations, other affiliated stations, and cable companies. As technology improved, we found that by compressing the uplink signal to the satellite we could get 12 programs on one transponder. This meant we were getting Worship and Paxson Communications (along with several others) on one transponder and disseminating the signals to all of our television stations and other affiliates.

As the date for launching Pax Net got closer I had an inner urge to review the satellite contract with Pan Am Sat. Though it was relatively inexpensive for satellite transponder time, there was something in me that said we needed to look at it. While Galaxy 6 had worked well, its transponder did not have a spot beam that would deliver signals to Hawaii, where we had just purchased a station, or Alaska, where we were lining up affiliates. I had received a proposal from Pan Am Sat to switch to a more powerful transponder on Galaxy 4, a satellite that would reach Hawaii and Alaska, but they had not yet gotten us a written contract.

Several weeks went by and we received an attractive proposal from GE Americom that would also cover our Hawaii and Alaska markets. They had heard we were looking for satellite space and a friend of mine from GE Americom called and reminded me of the relationship I had with them when I was with Home Shopping. Since I had not been able to get a contract with Pan Am Sat, I said, "OK, you have a deal!" I had the GE contract in less than a day. Obviously, now I had duplicating signals on two satellites, Galaxy 6 and GE Americom. My original intention with Pan Am Sat was to trade in our space on Galaxy 6 for the new space on Galaxy 4. Now I needed to sell the transponder on Galaxy 6 and I thought I knew who I might sell it to. Meanwhile, our costs for satellite transponders had gone from almost $80,000 a month to more than $180,000 a month. My executives at PCC thought I had lost my mind.

Then on May 15, Galaxy 4, on which I originally was to

have the new transponder, fell out of the sky. That satellite carried the signal for ninety-five percent of all the pagers in the country. Doctors and hospitals were thrown into chaos. Television stations scrambled to get their programs back on the air. I saw immediately why the contract had been delayed. Had the paperwork been processed, as it should have been, we would have had all our programs on Galaxy 4. After the satellite failure, we would have been off the air and would have been looking for a new transponder. God was protecting us from that mistake.

It never entered my mind that it was a coincidence. It was a clear message from the Lord that he was still with us in this venture.

But that is only half the story. When Galaxy 4 fell, Pan Am Sat had to find 24 new homes for the leases that were on the fallen satellite. Under the terms of our agreement back in 1991, they had the right to kick off the Christian Network from Galaxy 6 if such a crisis occurred. So on Wednesday, Dusty Rubeck, the president of CNI, got the call that by 3:00 that afternoon, all programming would be off the air. I called GE Americom and they said, "Don't worry about it. We can put you on the new satellite right now." They switched us that day and our viewers never missed a program. By preempting us off Galaxy 6, Pan Am Sat was cancelling our obligation for the then current contract. Not only did God stop the contract on the old satellite that would have run through the year 2004, he saved us from going off the air altogether.

Before this incident, I hadn't seen a specific blessing from God in a while. However, I wasn't worried, because I had seen God's intervention so many times in the past. But just a week before, I began to pray, "God, I know you are in this and I trust what you are doing, but it sure would be nice to see your hand clearly." Then, a week later—Boom!—a satellite fell from the sky. I felt very blessed.

IMAGINE WHAT THE END MIGHT LOOK LIKE

Every dream takes on its own life. Allowing it to grow begins with a mental image of what the dream *might* look like. The word "vision" evokes images and pictures and causes us to imagine an ideal situation. It speaks of something that's unique. A vision could be defined as *an ideal and unique image of the future* (*The Leadership Challenge,* p. 84). A visionary leader is someone who has been captured by an idea and a unique dream of the future and is able to infect others with that dream.

I like to think of visionary leaders as people who always carry a pair of binoculars. Rather than spending their time looking at the world through a magnifying glass, they view it through binoculars. They look at the horizon, put their binoculars down, and point others in that direction. *They do not follow where the path may lead. Instead, they go where there is no path and leave a trail.*

It's easy to get caught in the trap of the present. We can become consumed doing things that are unimportant. I'd urge you to periodically pick up an imaginary pair of binoculars and look into your future. Where would you like to be in two years? Or five? Or ten?

As you evaluate your potential future, remember the importance of balancing the business side of your life with the spiritual. What values do you want to live with through your endeavors? Remember, the greatest challenge we face is getting three threads of life through the eye of the needle: the business thread, the spiritual thread, and the family values thread. If we focus exclusively on one thread, the other two will fall out of place. I know because I've lived it. I concentrated for years on just the business thread and lost the other two. Successful living requires dreaming about not only *what* we will become in the business world, but *who* we will become and what values we will express through our endeavors. A dream that is apart from God transforms itself into a nightmare.

CULTIVATE A CREATIVE IMAGINATION

Developing the ability to imagine what a dream could look like involves the cultivation of our imagination. How important is imagination? Napoleon said, "Imagination rules the world." Einstein observed, "Imagination is more important than knowledge, for knowledge is limited to all we now know and understand, while imagination embraces the entire world, and all there ever will be to know and understand."

Visionary leaders use their imagination to draw detailed plans in their mind. They imagine as much detail as possible. That's what I did when I wrote the nonprofit business plan for *Worship*. I dreamed about a program that would allow a viewer to see God's work and grasp His love. Later, as that dream became a reality, it has expanded and is aired over a vast network of television stations here in the United States and around the world. Each step along the way, as the dream expanded, I worked hard to discern God's will, clearly identifying as many details of the vision as possible. Why? So that I could successfully flesh out the dream the way God wanted it to develop.

Such mental discernment of God's will is crucial. We're living in a day when imagination is a priceless commodity. Because our world is changing so fast, we must carefully cultivate our imagination. According to Tom Peters, author of *Liberation Management* and co-author of *In Search of Excellence*, we're living in the midst of a once-every-two-hundred-year major revolution. The technological revolution brought about by the growth of the computer is transforming the world at an amazing speed.

"Since 1979, when Sony Corporation invented the Walkman," wrote Stephen Brull in the *International Tribune* in March 1992, "the company has developed 227 different models, or about one every three weeks" (quoted in *The Tom Peters Seminar,* Tom Peters, Random House, New York, 1994, p. 6).

In 1981, nearly three thousand new products made their way to the grocery and drugstore shelves in the United States. Just a decade later, in 1991, that number soared to 16,143. That's the equivalent of a new product being introduced every half hour a year (*ibid.,* p. 18).

Because our world is changing so quickly, it desperately needs visionary leaders who are willing to use their imagination. The greatest dreams you can imagine will find their source in your greatest passions. Because I have tried to filter my dreams through God's will, He has helped turn my dreams into reality.

3

LIVE THE DREAM

In 1947 Jackie Robinson became the first African-American to play in major league baseball. I think it's reasonable to look back at his impressive career and note why he broke through an invisible race barrier that others couldn't penetrate. Certainly his exceptional athletic ability played a major role, but there was something else that set him apart from others. Jackie Robinson had a passion for the game of baseball and would not rest until he lived his dream of playing in the major leagues.

"It won't be easy," said Branch Rickey of the Brooklyn Dodgers. "You'll be heckled from the bench. They'll call you every name in the book. The pitchers will throw at your head. They'll make it plain they don't like you, and they'll try to make it so tough that you'll give up and quit." Then he added sternly, "But you won't fight back, either. You'll have to take everything they dish out and never strike back. Do you have the guts to take it?" (Hal Butler, *Sports Heroes Who Wouldn't Quit,* New York: Simon & Schuster, 1973, p. 46.)

Jackie Robinson had the "guts" to endure because he had the courage to dream something others had ridiculed. Did his passion for the game pay off? In 1947 he became the National League Rookie of the Year and in 1949 the Most Valuable Player, eventually entering baseball's Hall of Fame with a lifetime batting average of .311.

In 1974, the city of Pasadena erected the Jackie Robinson Center in his old neighborhood. In that setting, Jackie Robinson, though dead, continues to provide opportunities where other young players can realize their dreams.

Step Two: Stir Up Your Passion

In the last chapter, we saw the importance of growing a dream. Now we're ready to consider step two. If you stop and think about great leaders, you'll probably be able to identify their passions. What was the passion of Martin Luther King, Jr.? Abraham Lincoln? Mother Teresa?

Every great leader has a passion that he or she pursued. Our problem is that the disappointments and the busy-ness of life can cause our passion to become dormant. Like a hibernating bear, passion sleeps harmlessly while the rest of life goes on.

God has uniquely wired each of us to possess special desires and aptitudes. The vision you have for your life, family, and career can be expressions of your God-given passion. Take the time to routinely pray and daydream about what you would be doing if you could have your cake and eat it too. What would your life look like if you were doing what you wanted to do? What would you be doing if you implemented your dreams? Keep in mind to daydream with God at your side.

Visionary leaders are change masters. They see the way things are and move forward to change them. Open the door to your God-given dreams and let them out. Turn them loose. That's what I did when I left HSN. I dreamed about my passion to communicate that God loves people, and from that dream the reality of PAX NET eventually came into being. When we started, God only allowed us to see *Worship*. We had to work and wait years before God showed us His plan for PAX NET, a new family-oriented television network.

Step Three: Share the Dream

At some point the vision has to be shared with a broader circle of people. When I began talking publicly about my dream for a new television network that would provide family programming, few saw the need. After all, they reasoned, the Family Channel already filled that niche, and certainly America did not need another TV network. When I spoke of buying stations all over the country first and then coming up with programming later, the experts questioned my unconventional approach. They based their concerns on the fact that nobody had ever done it that way before. ABC, CBS, NBC, Fox, WB, and UPN had developed programming first and then found affiliate stations who would air their programming.

Of course, such concerns have been voiced before. When Ted Turner and Allen Neuharth announced their plans for new business ventures—Turner to begin an around-the-clock news television channel and Neuharth to start a national daily newspaper—people raced to the talk-show circuit so they could be the first to pronounce their ventures would fail. They both had a crowd of skeptics who doubted their every move.

Yet these two men believed their dreams. Even during the first years, when CNN and *USA Today* were losing millions of dollars, Turner and Neuharth refused to doubt their dreams. They didn't panic and they didn't question the ultimate success of their ventures.

Their success is now history. Both CNN and *USA Today* transformed and redefined the news industry. Why? Because these two men had dreams that required an unconventional never-before-tried approach that they refused to give up on. While the approach of Paxson Communications was unconventional, it too will succeed because, I believe, PAX NET is God's plan for us and our company.

RALLY THE TROOPS

Visionary leaders not only imagine what could be and seek to bring it into reality, they rally other people around their dreams. They cause people to find significance in performing the most mundane tasks because those tasks are essential for the accomplishment of the dream. I believe people are looking for something that will give their life meaning. Skilled leaders impart a vision that does just that. They enable others to feel their life matters because they are linked with an important cause.

As you seek to develop your ideas, you'll discover there are plenty of dream robbers—individuals and circumstances that will discourage you. Overcoming these dream robbers is almost impossible to do alone. That's why you'll need to surround yourself with God's love and guidance and lots of fellow dreamers.

SURROUND YOURSELF WITH DREAMERS

I've always enjoyed the humorous reminder that there are three kinds of people in the world: those who make things happen, those who watch things happen, and those who sit around and say, "What happened?" I laugh when I hear those words because I've known people who fit into all three categories, and I know the importance of surrounding myself with those who make things happen—people like Martha Williamson and Della Reese.

Martha, the executive producer of *Touched by an Angel*, likes to tell the story about the all-important insurance physical exam she and Della Reese had to undergo before they could begin shooting the series. That entertaining experience convinced her that Della is more than a great actress. She is also a great dreamer.

While Martha waited to be examined, Della was in a second examination room. After Martha had sat, barely clad, for a lengthy period of time, a nurse opened the door and stepped into her room. The nurse was visibly nervous and spoke in a hushed tone, "Miss Williamson, we have a problem with Miss Reese."

That was not good news and Martha was understandably alarmed. She knew they were both being examined by a "showbiz doctor." These were physicians retained by insurance companies to confirm the health of stars and key executives before the beginning of a television show. Showbiz doctors, according to Martha, weren't known for their comprehensive physicals. The word around Hollywood was that if a patient was alive and able to stand they had a good chance of being approved for an eighty-hour work week. Therefore, if the doctor was concerned, something really bad must have been wrong with Della. At that moment Martha feared her career as a key executive would be short-lived.

As her mind swirled with such pessimistic thoughts the nurse went on: "Miss Reese refuses to sign her insurance form."

Initially, Martha thought Della didn't want to reveal her age. But that didn't make much sense, since nothing about that robust woman had ever led Martha to think she would shy away from revealing her date of birth. No, Martha knew there had to be something else going on.

Once more the nurse interrupted Martha's thoughts. "In the blank where it says 'Anticipated Length of Employment,' I wrote 'six episodes.' Miss Reese won't sign it until I change it to say 'ten years.' She says it's 'a God thing.'"

Only a few days earlier, Della's star had been placed right outside on the Hollywood Walk of Fame. Time and again Della had said she believed in herself, but on this day she stood up in her paper gown and said she believed in Martha Williamson.

Martha, who had dreamed of a show that would tell people that God loved them, knew in a moment that Della Reese had a dream of her own. Della Reese believed God had brought them all together and her vision was of a show that would last at least ten years.

"I guess you'd better change the form," Martha told the nurse. "If Della says ten years, then that's what we ought to plan on." (Adapted from *Touched by an Angel* by Martha Williamson and Robin Sheets, Zondervan Publishing House, Grand Rapids, MI, 1997, pp. 16–18.)

If you want to dream dreams that are bigger than you could fulfill yourself, then surround yourself with other people who aren't afraid to dream the impossible. People like Della Reese, who refused to settle for less than the dream God had planted in her heart. These are the individuals who will buoy your spirit and enable you to persevere in the face of adversity and the dream robbers.

Step Four: Bring the Dream into Reality

I opened the last chapter by telling you about the important ruling all of us at Paxson Communications were waiting for. If the highest court in the land upheld the *must carry* law, then our stations would have a chance to be viewed easily in every major market in the United States.

What I didn't tell you was how, prior to that critical moment, God had made it clear he was with us in the creation of PAX NET. In the summer of 1994 the Supreme Court conducted its first review of the *must carry* law, enacted by Congress in 1992, and our company was buying its third TV station, in Atlanta. The station was costing us $9 million. We had just signed the agreement to purchase it, following FCC approval, and escrowed 10 percent of the purchase price.

The evening after making the escrow deposit, I panicked. I had a bad case of buyer's remorse. I had perched our company at the end of a flimsy economic limb. If we failed to quickly make this station profitable, it could bring down the whole company.

For several days I was overcome with worry. During the third sleepless night I turned on the TV to watch *Worship*. I had decided to take my own advice and share my fear with God. With *Worship*'s programming filling the room and creating an atmosphere for prayer, God almost immediately filled my heart with a knowing. I couldn't shake the knowing, and it grew until all doubt was gone. The knowing from God was, "Don't worry about *must carry*." (In Chapter Nine I'll talk more about this and share with you some specific principles that I've found helpful in discerning God's will.)

After this experience I realized God was with us and aggressively moved forward with the purchase of additional stations. As March 1997 approached I knew the ruling had to be announced soon. I also knew that every Monday morning at 10 A.M. the decisions were posted on a bulletin board in the lower lobby of the Supreme Court. So every Monday morning I sent someone with a cell phone over to the lobby so I could get the decision as soon as it was posted.

At precisely 9:45 A.M. on Monday morning, March 31, 1997, I got a call from a lawyer—but not from my associate waiting at the Supreme Court. The attorney had somehow gotten word from a reliable source that the ruling had supported *must carry*.

I wanted to call my guy in Washington so I could verify what I had heard. But I didn't have the number to his cell phone. It just so happened that I was having a staff meeting at ten in the morning. Four minutes after ten the doors to the conference room swung open and Tony Morrison, our vice president and general counsel, said, "We got the call."

For a brief moment it seemed as if time stood still. It only took a second for him to deliver the next part of the message, but it seemed like an eternity as a thousand thoughts and emotions raced through my mind. We all held our breath. No one spoke. No one moved. You literally could have heard a pin drop as we waited for the next words.

"The United States Supreme Court upheld 'Must Carry'!"

Once Tony had uttered those final eight words, all twenty of us in the room started to cry. We were like a bunch of kids who had just won an Olympic gold medal. I called my wife and told her to gather up some party trappings and bring them to the office. "We're going to celebrate." And celebrate we did—and pray we did. We gave thanks to God and celebrated his grace. We knew that *he* had prepared us for that moment.

BELIEVE THE DREAM

I realize there are plenty of doubters out there—people who think our dream of a family-oriented network that tells people God loves them will fail. But I'm convinced PAX NET can't fail. How can it? God has shown his presence in our endeavors time and time again. He is with us.

We own and operate more than seventy-five television stations, which reach most of the U.S. market. Nobody operates as many stations as we do.

What most people don't realize is that networks like Warner Brothers and UPN have only affiliate stations, which are independently owned. These stations air Warner Brothers or UPN programming. The WB and UPN networks provide only between nine and twelve hours of programming to each affiliate station every week. In order to fill those hours WB and UPN spend hundreds of millions of dollars a year on programming. Their network advertising revenue does not come close to paying for their programming. That means WB and UPN lose money every year on their affiliate stations that are independently owned.

That bit of information causes most people to ask, *Well, then, how do they make so much money?* The major networks like CBS, NBC, ABC, and Fox make their profits off the few stations they own themselves, not the network. If WB or UPN owned most of their affiliate stations, they could be raking in hundreds of millions of dollars in profit a year.

The key to making money in television is in owning the stations, not creating programming and only selling network advertising. PAX NET has introduced a new economic paradigm. We bought the affiliate stations before we bought the programming. We did it backward. Why? *As the owner of all the stations, PAX NET will receive all of the revenue from the sale of network, national spots, and local advertising.*

Obviously, good programming is vital. PAX NET owns the syndication rights to some of the best shows ever created: *Touched by an Angel; Dr. Quinn, Medicine Woman; Promised Land; Dave's World; Diagnosis Murder; Life Goes On;* and other top-line family-oriented shows. Seven days a week the American public will be able to turn on their television and watch these great shows.

I'm convinced my dream from God will become a reality. But what about your dreams? Have you reviewed them with God? As you work through the process of identifying your dreams and sharing them with others, you'll need to be ready to take the next step. You'll need to be ready to grab the opportunities that will come your way, so your dreams can become a reality. If you want to discover how to do that, turn the page.

4
SEIZE THE OPPORTUNITY

Webster tells us that an *opportunity* is "a favorable juncture of circumstances." In other words, an opportunity occurs when the elements needed for progress come together at the same time.

Seizing these opportunities is crucial. Philosopher George Santayana once said that those who do not study history are condemned to repeat it. While his words are on target, I think there is a more ominous danger. I'm speaking about the danger encountered by those who do not see the shape of the future. They don't run the risk of repeating yesterday's mistakes, but of missing tomorrow's opportunities.

Too often leaders base their decisions on past history rather than future opportunity. Bob Murley was a very dear Christian friend who helped me during a difficult time in my life. He would often recite this profound truth: "*On the plains of hesitation bleach the bones of countless millions; when given an opportunity, they sat down to contemplate it, and there they died.*"

Earlier I noted that I didn't find success, it found me. I don't mean that I sat around waiting for opportunity to knock on my front door. I mean the greatest opportunities I have encountered weren't the ones I went looking for. Instead, while doing something as seemingly mundane as collecting money from delinquent accounts, I saw an opportunity to sell merchandise over the radio and was able to see the potential for TV. Visionary leaders are not so trapped by the way things have always been done that they miss the opportunities that stare them in the face.

All of the success I've experienced in the business world has occurred because I grabbed opportunities that others didn't see. Or, if they saw them, they waited too long and the "juncture of favorable circumstances" passed. History is filled with the stories of men and women who looked into the future and saw what could be. Instead of waiting, they seized the opportunity and changed the world.

There are those who believe opportunity is nothing more than being in the right place at the right time. Others would say opportunity is another word for luck. I believe many of the strategic opportunities we encounter come directly from the hand of God. By seizing them we please God and, in turn, he places us in situations where we can grow and develop—situations where we can thread the needle by tapping into the grace of God as we consciously seek to please him. Whatever your belief, it's vital to see opportunities in light of your personal goals and values. As a Christian, I must always consider what God would want and how an opportunity might enable me to play a role in His larger plan.

With every opportunity also comes the responsibility to develop it. All it takes is one good opportunity to transform your life and world. Since that's the case, I want to share with you some principles that are crucial to making the best of good opportunities.

LOOK INTO THE FUTURE

Radio was my first business love. I was only a kid when I opened the front door of our house in Rochester, New York, walked down the sidewalk, and made a right-hand turn. I didn't stop walking until I arrived at the local radio station. I was only fourteen years old when I was spinning records as a Saturday-morning disc jockey for a show called *Kiddie Go*

Round. I worked my way through Syracuse University as an announcer, and shortly after graduation I was ready to step into the field of ownership and management.

It didn't take long for an opportunity to come along. In 1957, at the age of twenty-two, I bought my first radio station in Newark, New York, just east of Rochester.

In 1991, after leaving HSN, I pursued my dream of developing *Worship.* One day, Jim Bocock, a senior vice president at HSN, called me on the phone and reminded me that we had talked about our mutual love for radio for over six years.

"Buy a station," he said.

"Yeah, I'll buy it and you run it."

"You've got a deal," he said.

After nine years at HSN, I was back in the radio business. At the time I bought the station I was thinking it would give me something to do while developing *Worship.* It would provide me a place to hang my hat.

In September 1991, we bought our first station, in Jacksonville, Florida. About the time we were going through Federal Communications Commission (FCC) approvals prior to closing the transaction, I asked Jim when he was moving to Jacksonville. He informed me he wasn't going to move. He was going to stay in Tampa, Florida.

"I thought you were going to run the station," I said.

"I'll run it from here," he replied.

"Exactly how much salary do you expect to get?" I asked.

After he told me the figure, I said, "We can't afford that. We'll just have to buy another one. If you can manage one you can manage two."

At about that time, while visiting in Washington, D.C., I learned of a potential rule change by the FCC that would have dramatic effects on the radio industry. The FCC was considering permitting station owners to own four stations in a city or market area instead of two. I sensed God was urging me to take advantage of my knowledge of the future—knowledge that provided me with a strategic opportunity. We wouldn't just buy two stations in a city, we'd buy all we could.

With 58 percent of the nation's 11,000 radio stations losing money in 1991, prices were depressed. Instead of the twelve to fifteen times future cash flow of the late 1980s, I found stations selling for five to seven times future cash flow and way less if they weren't profitable.

In those markets where we bought the legal limit of two stations, we signed agreements with competitors that allowed us to manage their stations for a fee. In the management agreements, we included options to buy the stations in the event of the FCC rule change. Because we could buy them cheaper, Jim and I chose to buy mostly losers.

Sure enough, in September 1992, the FCC made the change in the multiple-ownership rule, and we moved quickly and bought the stations with which we had management agreements and options. We were able to turn these stations around financially because we consolidated management. Instead of four bookkeepers, we had one; instead of four general managers operating one station each, we had one operating four. We saved money in every area except "on-air" personalities. Plus, by owning four stations in a market we could offer advertisers package deals that were cheaper than buying airtime from separate stations.

Did my willingness to look into the future and act on the opportunities it offered pay off? Without a doubt! I believe it was God's plan for us to prosper in radio on a grand scale. In 1991, during the first year of operations, Paxson Communications had revenue of $650,000. In 1992, revenue shot up to $17 million and nearly doubled to $32 million in 1993.

The importance of not allowing the past to prevent you

from acting on what you perceive the future to hold is crucial. A while back I ran across a letter that allegedly was written over 165 years ago by Martin Van Buren to President Jackson. The letter resists the changes that new railroads would introduce to the United States. Historians may debate the authenticity of the letter, but its tone is strikingly similar to contemporary naysayers who base their decisions about the future on the past.

January 31, 1829

To: President Jackson:

The canal system of this country is being threatened by the spread of a new form of transportation known as "railroads." The federal government must preserve the canals for the following reasons:

One. If canal boats are supplanted by "railroads," serious unemployment will result. Captains, cooks, drivers, hostlers, repairmen, and lock tenders will be left without means of livelihood, not to mention the numerous farmers now employed in growing hay for horses.

Two. Boat builders would suffer and towline, whip and harness makers would be left destitute.

Three. Canal boats are absolutely essential to the defense of the United States. In the event of the expected trouble with England, the Erie Canal would be the only means by which we could ever move the supplies so vital to waging modern war.

As you may well know, Mr. President, "railroad" carriages are pulled at the enormous speed of fifteen miles per hour by "engines" which, in addition to endangering life and limb of passengers, roar and snort their way through the countryside, setting fire to crops, scaring the livestock, and frightening our women and children. The Almighty certainly never intended that people should travel at such breakneck speed.

> *Martin Van Buren*
> *Governor of New York*

Please understand, when Governor Van Buren sent that letter he was serious. What caused his concern? He had a fixation with the past that prevented him from seeing the opportunities of the future. No barrier to your future success is more important to overcome than this one. Look to the future for the opportunities that you can seize. As you do that, you'll be ready to take the next step.

EVALUATE THE OPPORTUNITY

Not every opportunity that presents itself is worthy of your attention. But if you encounter one with potential, evaluate it as thoroughly and quickly as time and resources allow. Also, always evaluate it from God's perspective. Does it fit in His overall plan? Is it something you believe he wants you to do?

This past year I was at a TV convention in New Orleans with Dean Goodman, the president of PAX NET. After dinner we went to a beautiful old hotel and Dean noticed a cigar with a $125 price tag. Because we saw that as an opportunity to sample a choice cigar, we each bought one. It was called Opus X and it was superb.

A short time later Dean was in Miami and visited a cigar store, where he asked for an Opus X. The proprietor smiled and said he had a few in his humidor.

"What do they cost?" Dean asked.

"They're $18 each."

I tell that story because it illustrates the fact that every opportunity that comes your way isn't one that should be taken advantage of. We only lost $107 each by paying too much for the cigars. But sometimes failing to evaluate an opportunity can cost much more in terms of time *and* money.

While at Home Shopping I learned that a major American publishing house had Bibles printed in Korea. I thought we might have an opportunity to work a great deal by going directly to the supplier. In order to check out the potential of the deal, I went to Korea on one of my buying trips and met with the owner of the printing company.

I realized right away that he was filling orders by printing a specific number of Bibles for the American publisher and then turning off his equipment. I suggested he leave the ink and paper in the machinery and continue the run until he had exhausted all the raw materials. I offered to purchase the end run for $3 each. Before long the printer was running an additional 10,000 Bibles and selling them to me at a discount. I, in turn, sold them over television for $7 each, just $1 more than the publisher's cost.

When the publisher got wind of this, he bought one of ours and realized it was exactly the same Bible. He called, dumbfounded that I could sell them so cheap.

In that instance I checked out an opportunity and it proved to be a great moneymaker for HSN.

DON'T GET SIDETRACKED

Once you've evaluated an opportunity and decided to pursue it, keep focused. Nothing will prevent you from moving forward like getting sidetracked on frivolous concerns. I refuse to allow my companies to get sidetracked on activities that divert resources away from our primary mission–to grow profitably.

For example, a number of years ago I entered into a contract with a business partner regarding how we would share the profits from the sale of two television stations. At the closing he demanded a share of the profits that was four times the original agreement. I had to make a choice—either let the deal fall through or give in to his demands.

My attorneys told me to sue him. My friends told me to sue him. My business associates told me to sue him. But I didn't sue him. Instead, I paid him most of what he demanded. Why? Because I didn't have time to waste in court. While I'm giving depositions and watching over a lawsuit, strategic opportunities are missed. Instead of focusing my energy on the next deal, I'm trying to recover from the exhaustion of a drawn-out trial. Rather than being out in the marketplace making deals, I'm sitting in a courtroom listening to lawyers argue. It's a waste of time. If your game is commerce, stay out of court.

Make no mistake about it, our company retains the best legal counsel available. But I will not waste my attorneys' time in court if it can be avoided. I refuse to squander important resources fighting over something with an uncertain outcome.

I'd rather go on to the next deal and forget about how somebody's greed drove him or her to forget their principles. How many times have I had to do that in the last ten years? A lot!

CHANGING COURSE

I've been criticized for changing course in midstream. But what people don't understand is that when a strategic opportunity comes along, I'm not going to turn it down just because it would mean changing course. One of my favorite sayings is: "There's nothing permanent but change." Once people realize that, they'll be in a better position to seize opportunities before they pass them by.

There are also situations where I've realized I needed to change course because the path I was on wouldn't get me where I wanted to go. When the HSN went public in 1986, it was one of the hottest offerings ever. By 1990, the stock had plunged. The company had spent over a year in a time-consuming, contentious, and expensive lawsuit. Competitors moved into the business. And as sales stalled, I tried to persuade my partner to forget about the suit. He couldn't and I'm convinced if we had done that HSN would be pulling in $10 billion in annual sales today.

Because I disagreed with some strategic business decisions the company made, I felt uncomfortable with its direction. When I figured out I couldn't change the future direction of HSN, I planned an exit. Also, at the same time I was going through a spiritual metamorphosis and felt I needed a change in order to progress personally. I knew that my relationship with Roy Speer and my productive years at HSN were over, and so I pulled out.

Knowing when to change course by pulling out is crucial. By staying in the wrong place I would have missed the media opportunities that have come my way. But, more importantly, I would have missed God's plan.

UTILIZE *STUPID SPEED*

Once you've identified an opportunity and decided to pursue it, don't waste a second. Utilize what I call *stupid speed*. Some of the best opportunities develop with lightning speed and require equally quick reaction. Those who are paralyzed by fear of failure will miss them every time. Don't worry about making small mistakes. If God is assisting and guiding you, He will help correct the mistakes.

People familiar with what we've done over the last several

years are astounded at the speed with which we operate our company. From 1991 to 1997 we assembled a forty-seven-station radio empire through the acquisition of the largest group of radio stations and radio networks in Florida. Since late 1993, we've made history by purchasing more television stations and building them from construction permits faster than anyone else has ever done. And we've positioned PAX NET to rapidly become a major player in network television. Today Paxson Communications owns more television stations than anyone else in the United States.

People wonder how we've done it. I'm prepared for such a fast pace of business because of the growth rate I learned at HSN. There, we'd put a product on the air and the viewers would order a hundred more than we had in stock. So we'd order an additional thousand. They'd buy those, and so we would buy an additional five thousand. We had incredible growth and we learned how to manage it by utilizing *stupid speed*.

In the spring of '97, I decided we should buy a major television station in New York for $257 million, and so I made a $25 million down payment. While we were planning to line up the money needed to close the purchase, Jim Carnegie, the editor of the *Radio Business Report*, called me on the phone.

"I hear you're selling your radio group," he said.

"I don't know where you heard that, but it's not true. I'm not selling. I need the cash flow from the radio group to borrow more money for TV station acquisitions. Where did you hear I'm selling?" I asked.

He said he had gotten the information from a reliable broker whom he didn't want to identify. His unwillingness to divulge his source annoyed me.

"You ought to tell me who he is because he's probably made a lot of money off me in the past," I said. "Now who is he?" I demanded.

Carnegie paused for a moment and then said, "It was Glen Serafin from Tampa. That's who told me you were interested in selling."

"Hold on a minute," I told him. "I'm going to set up a conference call with all three of us."

Once I had Glen on the phone I said, "Glen, where did you get the idea I wanted to sell my radio group?"

"Well," he stammered. "I didn't exactly say it like that."

"How did you say it?" I asked. "Mr. Carnegie has called me on the phone telling me I'm a candidate to sell, and I'm not. Now exactly what did you tell him?"

"Well, I just logically thought it was time that you might sell and I said so," he replied.

"I'm not a candidate to sell. No! Never! Nohow! Never! No!" I insisted.

We got off the phone and Mr. Carnagie published the story saying I wasn't interested in selling the radio group. He wrote it just as it happened. He described the conference call and everything.

Once the story appeared in *Radio Business Report,* every major radio station group buyer in America called me on the phone asking how much I would take for the radio group. Finally, I received a call from Lowry Mays of Clear Channel Communications, a highly regarded public company that is headquartered in San Antonio, Texas.

"Where's the bid on your radio group?" he asked.

"I'm not for sale," I said.

"Yes, you are," he said. "Come on, I know you are for sale."

"I'm not lying," I insisted. "I'm not for sale."

"You are too," he said. "I've done my homework and I know you'll sell for $600 to $650-odd million."

"You're serious. Aren't you?"

"Yes, I am," he said. This offer was out of the blue, and I immediately saw God's hand in it.

I told him I'd call him in a few days and hung up the phone. Immediately, I evaluated the opportunity. I had a number of big-time radio personalities whose vulgarity on the air bothered me and whom I wanted to get off my stations. My spirit was constantly troubled by raunchy radio. Selling the stations would solve that problem by handing them off to someone else. God has prospered us in radio and now wanted us to redeploy the monetary value of the radio stations.

Plus, managing the radio group took a tremendous amount of time. The forty-seven radio stations were making millions in profit, but I knew it was time to let go. And I knew the proceeds from the sale would be available for the New York television station—and other TV stations I intended to purchase. TV was God's plan.

So I picked up my phone and called Lowry.

"Six hundred million and what?" I asked.

"What do *you* want?" he said.

"Look, you're the only guy I'm talking with about the deal. So you tell me what you'll give for the radio group."

"I'll give you $633 million," he said.

"Okay."

"What do you mean by okay?" he asked.

I said, "I mean okay. I accept your offer."

In that moment I practiced *stupid speed*. How could I turn down such an offer? He had just offered me a price that was 19.7 times cash flow. At that time, it was the highest rate anybody ever sold a station group for in radio history. Plus, selling the stations solved a number of problems and provided revenue for the New York station and future TV opportunities.

NO EXCUSES . . . SEIZE THE OPPORTUNITY

Few stories illustrate the benefit of seizing the opportunity better than the true-life story of Walt Jones of Tacoma, Washington, as told by Bob Moawad. Walt outlived his third wife, to whom he was married for fifty-two years. When she died, someone said to Walt that it must be sad losing such a long-time friend. His response was, "Well, of course it was, but then again it may be for the best."

"Why was that?"

"I don't want to be negative or say anything, or defame her wonderful character, but she kind of petered out on me in the last decade."

When asked to explain, he went on to add, "She just never wanted to do nothin', just kind of became a stick-in-the-mud. Ten years ago when I was ninety-four, I told my wife we ain't never seen nothin' except the beautiful Pacific Northwest. She asked me what was on my mind, and I told her I was thinkin' about buying a motor home and maybe we could visit all forty-eight of the contiguous states. 'What do you think of that?'

"She said, 'I think you're out of your mind, Walt.'

"'Whydya say that?' I asked.

"'We'd get mugged out there. We'd die and there wouldn't be a funeral parlor.' Then she asked me, 'Who's going to drive, Walter?' and I said, 'I am, Lambie.' 'You'll kill us!' she said.

"I'd like to make footprints in the sands of time before I check out, but you can't make footprints in the sands of time if you're sitting on your butt . . . all you can make is buttprints in the sands of time."

"So now that she's gone, Walt, what do you intend to do?"

"What do I intend to do? I buried the old gal and bought me a motor home. This is 1976, and I intend to visit all forty-eight of the states to celebrate our bicentennial."

Walt got to forty-three of the states that year, selling curios and souvenirs. When asked if he ever picked up hitchhikers, he said, "No way. Too many of them will club you over the head for four bits or sue you for whiplash if you get into an accident."

Walt hadn't had his motor home but a few months and his wife had only been buried for six months when he was driving down the street with a rather attractive sixty-two-year-old woman at his side.

"Walt?" he was asked.

"Yeah," he replied.

"Who was the woman sitting by your side? Is she your new lady friend, Walt?"

To which he replied, "Yes, she is."

"Yes she is what?"

"My lady friend."

"Lady friend? Walt, you've been married three times, you're 104 years of age. This woman must be four decades younger than you."

"Well," he responded, "I quickly discovered that man cannot live in a motor home alone."

"I can understand that, Walt. You probably miss having someone to talk to after having had a companion all these years."

Without hesitation Walt replied, "You know, I miss that, too."

"Too? Are you inferring that you have a romantic interest?"

"I just might."

"Walt . . . "

"What?" he said.

"There comes a time in a person's life when you knock that stuff off."

"Sex?" he replied.

"Yes."

"Why?"

"Well, because that kind of physical exertion could be hazardous to a person's health."

Walt considered the question and said, "Well, if she dies, she dies."

Make no mistake about it, Walt Jones knew how to seize the opportunity. In 1978 with double-digit inflation heating up the country, Walt was a major investor in a condominium development. When asked why he was taking his money out of a secure bank account and putting it into a condo development, he said, "Ain't you heard? These are inflationary times. You've got to put your money into real property so it will appreciate and be around for later years when you really need it." How's that for grabbing an opportunity?

In 1980 he sold off a lot of his property in and around Pierce County, Washington. Many people thought Walt was cashing in his chips. He gathered his friends and told them he had sold off the property to increase his cash flow. "I took a small down and a thirty-year contract. I got four grand a month comin' in until I'm 138." (Jack Canfield and Mark Victor Hansen, *Chicken Soup for the Soul*, Health Communications, Inc., Deerfield Beach, FL, 1993, pp. 214–217.)

If Walt Jones, at 104 years of age, could seize the opportunities that came his way, doesn't it make sense that you can do the same thing with those you encounter? As you determine to seize the opportunities you face, you'll discover that one thing you need to bring it into reality is a strong team. In the next chapter I'll tell you how I've built a team. A team whose leader is God.

5

BUILD A WINNING TEAM

I'll never forget the brass vases we sold in pairs over the Home Shopping Network (HSN). Each stood eight inches tall and was suitable for displaying flowers on an entry table. Because we had bought sixty thousand we needed to get rid of them fast. All of them!

Of course, nobody in the viewing audience knew we had paid only $1 for each vase. In order to accentuate their beauty we pulled the camera in close enough so that each image filled the entire television screen. If a viewer had a fifty-inch screen, these vases looked pretty big. In fact, they looked like a real bargain at the price of two for $8.

Anyway, the host was pitching these vases on live television and hardly anybody was placing an order. I knew we had crate after crate of them piled up in the warehouse, and I knew we couldn't send them back to the manufacturer.

AUNT ESDA'S ASHES

As I was watching the show I suddenly got a brainstorm. I remembered that a relative, Aunt Esda, had recently died and been cremated. Her dying request was that her ashes be spread out over a wide area. It occurred to me that the United States covered a pretty wide area.

I immediately rushed up to the host, and in front of the cameras said, "You know, we're not doing a very good job selling these beautiful vases. I've been watching and I just had a thought. I'd like to ask the viewers to help me do a favor for an old friend, Aunt Esda. Aunt Esda died last month and asked that her ashes be spread all over America. Tomorrow I'm getting the urn with her ashes. I'm going to go into the warehouse and put one ash in every one of these vases."

I then looked into the camera with a serious gaze and somberly said, "Will you help me fulfill the dying wish of Aunt Esda? Will you buy a pair of these vases, and after unwrapping them take them outside and empty Aunt Esda's ashes onto a beautiful spot in your yard?"

The phones immediately lit up, and we sold all thirty thousand sets of those vases. Do you know what? Nobody believed a word I said, but we had fun together.

As a kid I used to visit the county fair. I remember the appeal of the carnival pitchman who would hawk his magic wax from a booth. From a microphone hanging around his neck he would bark out, "It will make your car shine. It will make your silver shine. It will make your floor shine. It will make your jewelry shine." The crowd would gather around to get a closer look at the miracle wax. People enjoyed being entertained by the pitchman. In a sense, I think HSN brought those qualities into the home through television. People love to watch the hosts hold up a piece of jewelry and pitch its attributes.

I've always had a unique ability to sell products and have fun doing it. On six or seven occasions I actually played that pitchman at HSN nonstop for twenty-four hours. Nobody has ever duplicated those Barg-A-Thon workdays.

"A SHOT OF RUM, PLEASE"

In the middle of the night, after I had been on the air for twenty hours straight, my voice would begin to fade. I discovered that a tiny shot of hot rum would anesthetize the pain and take away the hoarseness. I'd hold the shot of steaming rum in front of the camera and quickly down it. I'd then smile and begin to act a little tipsy. After a few minutes I'd pretend I had forgotten the price of a product.

"Now what was the price of that makeup case? Oh, forget it. Was it $30? Forget the $30. I'll sell it to you right now for $10." The viewers knew I was pretending to be tipsy and they played along with the idea that I was discounting items because I had been drinking. I wasn't drunk. It was just a fun game I played with the viewers.

I tell those stories because they illustrate the power of television to engage people in what's happening on TV. HSN is popular because the viewer actually interacts with what's taking place on the screen. They can call and talk with a host. They can buy the very product they see being sold. Obviously, when it comes to a pair of vases for $8 the American public is educated on the value of products enough to know a priceless heirloom can't be bought for a few dollars. Viewers are looking for a good deal, but they also enjoy participating in what's happening live on camera. It has to be entertaining and fun. Today, in my opinion, it's all pitch, and the fun is all but gone.

This uncanny instinct to read the American psyche has served me well in the past, and it continues to do so as the dream of PAX NET becomes a reality. I know that PAX NET will succeed because we'll provide what the American public wants.

But I also know that bringing the dream into reality is a bigger job than one man can pull off alone. Every visionary leader and deal maker needs a team of people to take advantage of his strengths and offer their strengths where he's weak. In this chapter I want to underline the importance of building a strong team, like the one we've pulled together at PAX NET.

BUILD ON YOUR STRENGTHS

Over the years I've been called a paradigm shifter. Thomas Kuhn introduced the term "paradigm shift" in his book *The Structure of Scientific Revolutions*. He observed that every significant breakthrough in almost any field begins with a break with tradition, with the old way of thinking, with old paradigms.

A paradigm shift occurs any time a light goes on in someone's head and he or she sees something in a fresh new way. My friend, author and motivational speaker Bill Perkins, likes to tell the story about a man who was driving his Mazda Miata down a winding country road one sunny spring day. As he was speeding around a turn, a woman in a big black Lincoln almost ran him off the road. Just as they sped by one another she leaned out her window and shouted, "Pig!"

Infuriated at the woman, he raised a clenched fist in the air and shouted something back at her. A moment later he rounded the curve and saw a three-hundred-pound pig standing in the middle of the road. As he careered his shiny red car around the pig, he saw things in a new way.

The history of innovation is marked by the stories of paradigm shifters. For years people laughed at the suggestion that clothes could be sewn with a machine. They said the notion was ludicrous. They called the idea absurd. After all, they reasoned, clothes have been sewn by hand for thousands of years. But Elias Howe saw something others didn't see. Since his invention of the sewing machine, the world has never been the same.

Another man, a college professor, wanted to provide his partially deaf sister with a hearing device to enhance her hearing. Instead of a hearing aid, he created something far more complex—an invention that would enable the human voice to travel for miles along a wire. After years of trial and error he

56

was ready to take his invention to production, and for years traveled throughout New England, trying to interest investors in his dream. They laughed at the thought. Nobody had ever done such a thing before. They couldn't imagine that the inventor actually believed the wire would carry the human voice for even *one* mile. While those would-be investors laughed, Alexander Graham Bell proved them wrong. Today nobody laughs at the ideas of Alexander Graham Bell. Instead, we all enjoy the benefits of his foresight.

I can identify with both Howe and Bell because my best ideas have been the ones people found the hardest to accept. They scoffed when I suggested products could be sold over the radio. But we did it. When we decided to sell merchandise over television, people said we were crazy. Yet the success of HSN is now history. The idea of a television station running infomercials during prime time seemed ludicrous. Nobody will watch an infomercial when they can watch a prime-time show, the critics insisted. Again history proved them wrong.

Frankly, I don't like the phrase "paradigm shifter." I prefer the word *pioneer*. A *pioneer* is someone who isn't afraid to blaze a trail where there is no path. He has the ability to see over the current horizon. He knows what is ahead and plans for the future as though it were the present.

I think of myself as a pioneer—or, if you prefer, a paradigm shifter. It's a tremendous asset to be able to see things in a fresh way. It enables me to introduce innovative and creative concepts, and then to have other talented people involved in the process of developing the ideas.

THE DEAL MAKER

A while back my son asked me to join him for a game of chess. I told him, "I can't play chess. It's too complicated. I don't know the rules." While I may not be able to play chess, I do know how to play the game of commerce. As I look over the United States and think of all of the television stations, it's the most complicated chess set you can imagine, but I know it intricately. I've been in television since the middle sixties and I have all the research tools in my hands. I know who owns the stations and what their assets look like. More importantly, I knew what needed to be done to assemble the most complete network of TV stations in the country.

Other players in the broadcasting chess game operate with only a few of the pieces. They may buy a station here or a station there. According to the June 30, 1997, issue of *Broadcasting & Cable,* the weekly publication for television and radio, Fox Television Stations had twenty-three stations, CBS had fourteen, NBC had eleven, and Walt Disney's ABC had ten. Paxson Communications has over seventy-five TV stations. How were we able to reach this historic figure? We did it because I dealt with the entire "board" of American television, not just a portion of it.

When I was with HSN I developed a friendship with two African-Americans, John Oxendine and Ed Parker. They owned a communications company named Blackstar, after the first slave ship. Television owners often sought members of minority groups to partner with them because for years minorities were given preference in acquiring new stations in markets. Around 1987, John and Ed went into a partnership with HSN. Television stations in Portland, Orlando, and Detroit would be in their names and HSN would loan them the money to build and operate the facilities. In return they agreed to affiliate and carry HSN programming twenty-four hours a day. HSN then paid them enough money monthly to operate the stations, repay the debt, and live a comfortable life. They ran the stations from a little two-man office in Washington, D.C.

After several years had passed, I was no longer with HSN and wanted to buy their Detroit station. John and Ed had become tired of waiting for a big payday, so they persuaded HSN to allow them to sell it to me. As we closed on the deal I told John I wanted to buy their Portland station as well. He made it clear HSN probably wouldn't allow them to sell the station.

Around the same time, a broker called me and said, "Bud, I know you have a station in Atlanta. Just in case you want to contract for a second one, I know where there's one that's about to go on the market. They want $10 million for it, which is cheap. But HSN is going to make an offer."

I realized at that time that if I could acquire the Atlanta station I would have a future bargaining chip with HSN. However, under FCC rules we could not own two TV stations in the same market. So, I made an arrangement with a friend: he would buy the station, but I would operate it.

Two months after that conversation, HSN sent the broker a contract to take to the owners of the Atlanta station, but they were too late. By the time HSN got around to making an offer I had already negotiated a contract with the owners and filed for approval with the FCC. Because I utilized *stupid speed* I was able to take advantage of a strategic opportunity that would have been gone quickly.

A year or so after striking the Atlanta station arrangement, I let HSN know that I was open to selling it. As I expected, they called me on the phone. "So you want to sell Atlanta, Bud?"

"Yeah, I might."

"Well, maybe we'd be interested in buying. We'll get back to you."

A month later they called again and said they wanted to buy the station. I told them, "I'll sell you Atlanta for $50 million, if you'll let me buy Portland for $30 million from Blackstar."

I had a plan! After doing the Atlanta station deal, I had contracted to buy two more TV stations that were HSN affiliates—one in Memphis and one in New Orleans. The only problem was that the HSN affiliation agreements wouldn't run out for two and a half years, and they dictated that HSN be carried for twenty-four hours a day. That meant that PAX NET programming couldn't air on those stations until the HSN affiliation agreement expired. Because I knew HSN wanted Atlanta, I sensed another opportunity to strengthen my position.

When HSN called me up and said they wanted to buy Atlanta I said, "Good. Terrific! Here's what I'll do. You pay me $50 million, I'll buy Portland for $30 million and give you $10 million to cancel the HSN affiliation agreements in New Orleans and Memphis."

Now remember, I bought the Atlanta station with the intent of using it to leverage HSN. Once they showed an interest in buying Atlanta, I realized I could also use the sale as an opportunity to get PAX NET on in Portland, in addition to New Orleans and Memphis, by buying out the HSN affiliation contract.

That was a great move because I paid only $10 million for the Atlanta station and then turned around and sold it to HSN for $50 million. With the profit from the sale I was able to buy Portland, free up Memphis and New Orleans, and had the original $10 million left over. Not a bad deal!

The problem is nobody on Wall Street understands all of this because they can't grasp the big picture. They don't understand that I've worked deals that are part of a much bigger plan—a plan that has gotten us into every major market for a fraction of what other networks have spent. That concept is still unfolding and will ultimately make PAX NET one of the financially strongest networks in television.

It's not arrogant for someone to recognize his or her strengths. However, it is a horrible arrogance to exaggerate them and false humility to minimize them. Threading the business needle involves running a business in a way that demonstrates vision. Such vision is exercised when a man or woman knows his or her strengths and builds a team that accentuates them. But it also involves knowing your weaknesses so team members can offer their strengths in those areas.

KNOW YOUR WEAKNESSES

While I'm skilled at seizing opportunities and making good deals, I'm not as gifted at making sure my strategy is being communicated to either Wall Street or the public. That reality hit home in November 1997, when Wall Street responded negatively to our announcement that PAX NET wouldn't partner with another company that would provide us with programming and additional money. Instead, we decided to buy programs, like *Touched by an Angel, Promised Land,* and *Dr. Quinn, Medicine Woman,* right from major studios and start a network of our own.

HIRE A P.R. FIRM

That news caused Paxson Communications stock to drop 35 percent. PaineWebber analyst Christopher Dixon said he found our approach, "intriguing," but he wasn't sure it was feasible. Smith Barney analyst John Reidy said my approach might be "doable," but he felt my assumptions on how much advertising time we could sell might be too "aggressive."

Others in Wall Street said I might sell PAX NET if the value of my formidable station group increased enough in value.

Observations like those created the impression that our approach was risky and the outcome uncertain. Instead of wringing my hands, I recognized my mistake and hired an investment and public relations firm, Brainerd, that specializes in dealing with Wall Street. They listened to our story and in a few months have done a better job communicating our strategy than I could do in a year. Brainerd is explaining our vision and strategy in a way that Wall Street understands, and our stock is slowly inching up again.

In addition, I appointed Seth Grossman to senior vice president of Investor Relations. I'm not going to deal with Wall Street alone anymore. I'm the visionary and deal maker. Seth is a master at fielding questions and communicating our vision. I don't have these attributes, so I found someone who could function in that role better than I could.

FIND A HUMAN RELATIONS EXPERT

Life would be a lot easier if each of us was born with an owner's manual that describes our strengths and weaknesses—a reference book that would tell us where we're a plus ten and where we're a minus ten. Unfortunately, we're given a blank book, and it's our job to fill it out.

A story is told of a highly successful bank executive who was retiring. As he cleared out his desk his young replacement stopped by for some words of advice.

"Mr. Jones, what's the key to your success? How have you been able to turn this bank, and others, from money losers into money makers?"

"Good decisions," the old man said gruffly.

"And how do you learn to make good decisions?"

"Experience."

"Where do you get the kind of experience that teaches you to make good decisions?" the young executive asked.

"Bad decisions," the old man said with a smile.

I wish I could say the old man is wrong, but he isn't. Nobody told me early on, "Bud, stick with being a visionary and coming up with fresh ideas and making deals." It never happened. I learned by making mistakes. That's how I discovered that I'm also not skilled at selecting good personnel. I'll go with my instincts every time when it comes to a deal, but if I do that with people I'm certain to make a mistake.

James Bocock, president of Paxson Communications, who has worked with me for about eighteen years, is just the opposite. Jim can look at people, talk to them a few minutes, and sense whether or not they're right for a job. He's not impressed with the superficial trappings that can mislead some people. Misreading someone can be very costly. Jim oversees the hiring of all key personnel for our company and is a genius at it. He has created a great management team at Paxson.

I like the story of the man who was sitting on a barstool drowning his sorrows when a good-looking dark-haired man sat down on the stool beside him. "Man, you look terrible," the handsome gent said. "What happened?"

"This has been the worst day of my life," the miserable man said. "I arrived at work only to discover I'd been fired. I went home and found all the furniture had been removed from my house. My wife left a note saying she had moved out and wasn't coming back. I called my dog and he was nowhere to be found. Eventually I discovered him lying beside the road. He had been hit by a car and killed."

The good-looking man placed a hand on the poor fella's shoulder and said, "Man, you have had a terrible day. I'll tell you what I do when I'm depressed. I climb to the roof of this building. There, fifty stories above the ground, I leap off the magical corner and free-fall toward the street. Just before I hit the street I magically stop and float back up to the roof. It's such an adrenaline rush that it totally reverses my depression."

"You're crazy," the depressed man said.

"I'll prove it to you," the dark-haired man said as he grabbed the distraught man by the arm and walked toward the door.

A few minutes later the two stood six hundred feet above the street. The handsome man positioned himself on the edge of the roof, spread his arms, and leaped into open space as his companion watched in disbelief. Sure enough, just before he hit the street, the man stopped and slowly floated back up to the roof.

"Wow! That was a rush!" he said. In order to convince his new friend, the man repeated the feat several times. "Try it," he said. "It will turn your bad mood around."

Convinced that the corner was indeed magical, the depressed man spread his arms and leaped into the air.

A few minutes later the handsome man with the dark hair strolled back into the bar and returned to the stool. The bartender looked him in the eye and said, "Superman, you're a real jerk when you've had too many."

While I've never misjudged someone that seriously, I have made more than my share of errors of judgment. Those mistakes have given me the experience to know that someone else on the team needs to make personnel decisions. I'm just not good at it.

Some of these personnel decisions are critical. For instance, several years ago we bought a station and later discovered that a key employee had likely been involved in some criminal activity. We didn't have time to deal with that kind of a mess.

Situations like that have taught us that the wisest thing to do when buying a station is have the former owner ask for everyone's resignation on the last day. We'll then evaluate the staff team and rehire those who will fit into our system of operating the station.

While this might sound heartless, it's in the best interest of both the employees and the station. No employee wants to get into a job situation where he or she can't succeed, and we don't want employees who will fail or be miserable.

Before we bought the TV station in Akron, Ohio, it employed eighty people. We bought and opened the station with thirteen employees. How can we do that? We can do it because in operating so many stations we've learned to consolidate the workplace and to streamline the workforce. In the process we have turned almost every station we bought into a moneymaker in a very short time.

Decisions like consolidation have to be made, but I don't personally make them. I leave them to the members of our team who specialize in employee relations. I'm the visionary, not the V.P. of Human Relations.

GET A COMPUTER SPECIALIST

Nothing has changed the world more than computers, and no field offers greater opportunities for the future than data management or the Internet. However, when it comes to actually using a computer, I'm all thumbs. In our home we have a television set linked directly to cable, a satellite, and a VCR. When I want it to work, I have to find my daugher, Nicole. I know I can't figure out how to use it. Instead of getting frustrated I just call Nicole.

At Paxson Communications we have a manager of information systems. While I understand the theory behind computers, I need someone else to manage that area of our company. The same is true in the field of accounting. I can read a balance sheet and analyze a profit-and-loss statement, but I don't fully understand the various principles of GAAP accounting. We have a chief financial officer, Arthur Tek, who oversees that segment of our business.

It's not enough for leaders to know their strengths. They must also know their weaknesses and recruit people who are strong where they are weak. That's what makes a team great.

BUILDING FOR THE FUTURE

There are times when I have felt that God was orchestrating personnel decisions long before I saw the need. Two of our most recent announcements involved people who came to us unexpectedly, and, in my opinion, through God's guidance.

I am always on the lookout for people with expertise and a philosophy that matches PAX NET's vision. So when I read that Jeff Sagansky had resigned as co-president of Sony Pictures Entertainment International, I was excited. I knew Jeff had produced *Highway to Heaven* when he was president of programming at NBC and later, as president of programming at CBS, had developed *Dr. Quinn: Medicine Woman* and *Touched by an Angel*. He certainly seemed to have an eye for the kind of shows we wanted to present at PAX NET. My first step was to call my friend Tony Molera, a consultant with Communications Equity (who had helped us get the show *Touched by an Angel*).

"Tony, do you know Jeff Sagansky?" I asked.

"Sure," he said, "I know him well."

"We would like to hire him as a consultant for our programming schedule. Can you set it up?"

Jeff and I got together to talk about what we were trying to do with the network. When I explained the economics of PAX NET owning our own stations and how that was the backbone of the network's success, he became very interested and saw that, unlike cable, we were starting with a distribution that took ESPN and TNT twenty years to build. Jeff felt that we would be profitable even if we could only get a 1 rating.

As we talked, we found that not only was PAX NET making sense to him economically, our philosophies about programming were almost identical, too. Jeff had been in the industry for many years. He had worked at CBS and NBC, and had been in on the start of Columbia TriStar Pictures. Obviously, he knew people in the industry and was connected to the inner circles of Hollywood. In May 1998, he accepted our offer as president and CEO of PAX NET under a four-year contract.

The same day we announced Jeff as our new president and CEO, we announced the appointment of Bill Simon, Jr., as vice chairman of the board of directors. Again, as I look back, I see how God was building our team at PAX NET long before the reality.

My first contact with Bill came in November 1997. He called and said he was interested in getting involved in Christian television and asked me to speak to my friend Leo Hindery at TCI, the largest cable provider in the country, about an association with Odyssey, a network owned (51%) by a group of sixty-five churches. I was reluctant to do so at the time because we were already in negotiations with TCI on a cable carriage deal. I had never met Bill and didn't hear anything more from him for several months.

In March 1998, an inquiry came to my desk, through one of our consulting firms, Communications Equity, that Bill Simon wanted to meet with me. I flew to Los Angeles and met with William Simon, Sr., the former secretary of the treasury under Nixon and Ford, and his son, Bill Simon, Jr., and members of their investment company, William T. Simon and Sons. We found we had a great deal in common and that Bill was very interested in what PAX NET was doing. Subsequently, he came to Florida and we spent a lot of time together sharing ideas and talking about the future of television.

Though Bill had a desire to change the face of Christian television, we both came to the conclusion that Christian television is not always "our utmost for His highest." Later, during the spring of 1998, the family made a $10 million investment in PAX NET and we named Bill, Jr., the vice-chairman of our board. Not only does he bring a strong financial voice to our company, he is also a perfect fit with our values and direction. While we were working to negotiate the deals to make PAX NET a reality, God was preparing people to help run the network and keep it close to His vision.

YOU'RE IMPORTANT!

In the final analysis, it doesn't matter how strong a leader may be, he or she must have a team of skilled players to win the game of commerce. How important is each member of the team? Or, to put it differently, how important are you? Several years ago the *Wall Street Journal* dedicated an entire page to the subject.

> **How Important**
> **Are You?**
> More than
> you think.
> A rooster
> minus a hen
> equals

no baby chicks.
Kellogg minus
a farmer
equals
no corn flakes.
If the nail
factory closes
what good is the
hammer factory?
Paderewski's
genius wouldn't have
amounted to much
if the
piano tuner
hadn't shown up.
A cracker maker
will do better
if there's a
cheesemaker.
The most skillful
surgeon needs
the ambulance driver
who delivers the
patient.
Just as Rogers
needed Hammerstein
you need someone
and someone
needs you.

In the final analysis, leaders who please God are those who
not only recognize their own strengths but their weaknesses as

well. Those are the leaders who will be able to utilize the strengths of others, so that together they can make a bigger difference than they could ever have made alone.

Yet, as a team pulls together, they'll discover there are those who want to rob them of their dream. In the next chapter, we'll discover how to deal with the dream robbers.

6
OVERCOMING THE DREAM ROBBERS

"You see things; and you say, 'Why?' But I dream things that never were; and I say, 'Why not?'" Those words by George Bernard Shaw capture the essence of visionary leaders. They have the unique ability to see possibilities where others see problems. But for every visionary who dreams of what could be, there are scores of dream robbers.

King Camp was a man with a dream. He believed his invention, a simple tool, could help millions of people. In the course of getting his invention on the market, he encountered numerous dream robbers. Everyone he showed the idea said it was cockeyed. No machinist would take on the project to make a prototype. Those experienced in the field, experts from Massachusetts Institute of Technology, said it couldn't be done. Investors turned him down without offering him a dime.

Fortunately, King Camp Gillette didn't allow any of his critics or opponents to rob him of his dream. They all said no one could make a razor sharp enough to give a good clean shave and cheap enough to be thrown away when it was dull. It took Gillette four years to produce the first disposable blade and six more to get it on the market. The first year Gillette sold fifty-one blades at $5 each. The second year, he sold 90,844 blades. Because he refused to allow the dream robbers to steal his dream, Gillette changed the way people shave.

I've mentioned on several occasions the presence of people

who can cause a visionary to give up the cause or get side-tracked—people like those Gillette had to deal with. I've certainly encountered my share of them.

A while back someone asked me, "Bud, did you ever get discouraged when you encountered the naysayers and others who tried to take the wind out of your sails?" Frankly, I didn't. I simply figured out how to strengthen our company and moved on. However, in the process I learned some principles that enabled me to move on more effectively—concepts that helped me defeat the dream robbers. In this chapter I'm going to identify the three kinds of dream robbers I've encountered. And then I'll share with you the strategies I've used to defeat them.

DREAM ROBBER ONE: THE CRITICS

Shortly after we announced our plans for PAX NET the critics almost stumbled over each other in an effort to predict our failure. Tony Vinciquerra, the executive vice president of Hearst/Argyle Television, which owns the Tampa-based WB Network affiliate, said, "Frankly, I'm baffled as to what he's going to do. The basic rule of TV is, you have to have good programming, get the signal to people who want it, and promote it heavily. Given those standards, it may be rough going for Paxson in the future." Bob Wright, president of General Electric's NBC, said, "He's just taking an absolute flier. I think it's probably a pretty high-risk venture."

When it comes to handling critics, I've found a four-step strategy that's proven helpful.

1. *Anticipate*

Nobody likes to be sucker-punched. Yet the only way to avoid such a blow is to expect it. The same is true of criticism. The most effective way to handle criticism is to know it's coming. Anybody who has the courage to move into uncharted waters needs to anticipate a host of naysayers who will forecast his or her failure.

I find it helpful to realize that many critics who are supposed to be experts aren't as expert at their predictions as they would like to believe. For instance, the managing director of the World Monetary Fund concluded in 1959, "In all likelihood world inflation is over."

Or how about Irving Thalberg, the MGM executive who warned Louis B. Mayer regarding *Gone With the Wind,* "Forget it, Louis, no Civil War movie ever made a nickel"? After Mayer took that advice he said, "Irving knows what's right." Mayer missed an opportunity of a lifetime. David O. Selznick produced the film in 1939.

In 1977, the president of Digital Equipment Corporation said, "There is no reason for any individual to have a computer in their home." Or how about the *Business Week* pro who in 1968 concluded, "With over fifty foreign cars already on sale here in the United States the Japanese auto industry isn't likely to carve out a big share of the market."

These quotes demonstrate that experts are frequently wrong. Because I know that, I refuse to let the doomsayers deter me when I'm convinced a course of action will bring success. Instead, I anticipate their criticism. Besides, many critics write for newspapers or magazines, and negative articles sell better; or so they think.

2. Assess

You might conclude that I deal with naysayers by expecting their criticism and then tuning it out. Such isn't the case. Instead, I listen to what they have to say and carefully assess it. Sometimes a critic will point out a legitimate issue or weakness that needs to be addressed.

For months prior to determining the future of our stations, we had been courted by the major networks—NBC, ABC, Sony, Turner, and others—who wanted to provide us with programming. During that time we indicated a partnership *might* be the route we would take. That was the word on Wall Street, and it was the word in the entertainment industry. When we decided to go it alone, our announcement shocked Wall Street and brought out the doomsayers.

I could have ignored the critics and said, "They don't know what they're talking about." Instead, I assessed what they were saying and concluded I had made a serious mistake, not in the business strategy but in our failure to communicate it. Instead of shocking the marketplace with the news of our plan to find our own programming, we should have educated Wall Street about our strategy. We should have let them know why we were moving in a different way.

3. Adapt

As I mentioned in the last chapter, that assessment prompted us to adapt by hiring an investment public relations firm that could more effectively communicate our strategy to Wall Street and the entertainment industry.

I like to compare such adjustments to the navigational device on a smart missile. During the Gulf War, Operation Desert Storm, most of us can remember the images we saw on television in which the missiles entered ventilation ducts in buildings. The accuracy of smart missiles is assured by a mechanism that allows a pilot to see the target through the eyes of the missile and actually direct the missile to the target. The pilot is continually adapting the trajectory of the missile, adapting to the environment and topography, so it will home in on the target.

Effective leaders learn how to do the same thing. They assess criticism and make whatever adaptations are needed so their company will hit the target. At PAX NET we've discovered that in most situations the criticism we experience isn't well founded. But even though we might know that, it's still wise to cultivate a willingness to adapt when necessary.

4. Move On

Regardless of whether or not we make any adaptations, we definitely move on once we've assessed the criticism. And we don't look back! I believe this final step is crucial in not allowing critics to rob you of your dreams.

Few men illustrate this principle better than Monty Roberts from San Ysidro, California. When Monty was a senior in high school, he was asked to write a paper about what he wanted to do with his life. That night he wrote a seven-page paper describing his goal of someday owning a horse ranch. He wrote about his dream in detail and even drew a diagram of a two-hundred-acre ranch, showing the placement of the buildings, the stables, and the track. He then sketched a detailed floor plan for a four-thousand-square-foot house that would sit on the ranch.

Two days after handing in the paper he received it back with a big red F on the top margin along with a handwritten note from the teacher—"See me after class!"

"Why did you give me an F?" he asked.

"Because your dream is unrealistic. You have no money. You come from an itinerant family. You have no resources. Owning a horse ranch requires a lot of money. You'll have to buy the land, pay for the original breeding stock, and later you'll have to pay large stud fees. There's no way you could ever do it. If you'll rewrite your paper with a more realistic goal, I'll reconsider your grade."

How did Monty respond to the teacher's criticism and concern? How did he respond to her lack of faith in him and his dream? He assessed her words. He talked with his dad. Finally, after considering her criticism for a week, he turned in the same paper without a single change.

As he handed it to the teacher he said, "You can keep your F and I'll keep my dream."

Having done that, Monty did something else. He moved on. In fact, today he lives in a four-thousand-square-foot house in the middle of his two-hundred-acre horse ranch. And what about the paper he handed in to the teacher? He had it framed and it now hangs over the fireplace in his ranch house.

You'd think this was the end of the story. It isn't. Several years ago that same teacher brought a class of kids to Monty's ranch. As she was leaving, she turned to Monty and said, "Look, Monty, I can tell you this now. When I was your teacher, I was something of a dream stealer. During those years I stole a lot of kids' dreams. Fortunately, you had enough gumption not to give up on yours." (Adapted from *Chicken Soup for the Soul,* Jack Canfield and Mark Victor Hansen, Health Communications, Inc., 1993, pp. 207–208.)

I applaud Monty and all those who refuse to allow the critics to steal their dreams. But there is a second dream robber that you need to be aware of.

DREAM ROBBER TWO: SETBACKS

Setbacks are different dream robbers from critics, and more dangerous. A setback occurs whenever something takes place that actually brings your business, or life, to a halt and then moves it back several steps. Once a setback occurs, you'll need to regroup, refocus, and restart. And the restart needs to be with a determination that that particular setback will never occur again.

I learned that last lesson the hard way. In February 1987 I could sense something was wrong at HSN. Until then our daily sales increases had steadily grown. Suddenly we were hitting a brick wall. People thought it was the annual post-Christmas drop. But I believed something else was taking place.

After extensive research we believed our telephone network and the switcher installed by our phone company had hit their capacity. Instead of fixing it, which would have been expensive, they tried to patch up the system.

Because one of our top executives had a legal background, he pressed hard for us to file a lawsuit against the phone company. At the time his experience convinced the rest of us that we should fight the matter in the courtroom and collect hundreds of millions in damages. We sued. They countersued.

The lawsuit involved HSN in a process that proved to be a huge setback. At the same time we sought to remedy the problem by building a new plant and installing an entirely new phone system and a new long-distance provider. Meanwhile, QVC merged with CVN and launched their program nationally. At a time when we encountered our stiffest competition, all of our mental and emotional resources were embroiled in a lawsuit.

The trial was a disaster for HSN. The lawyer for the phone company had a down-to-earth style that connected with the six-person jury. For eleven weeks we sat in a courtroom while this lawyer portrayed us in the worst imaginable terms. Over time, the jury grew to hate us.

During his closing summation, in Abe Lincoln style, their lawyer said, "You know, we've filed a lawsuit against those two guys for defamation. They damaged our company's reputation but we don't want their money; we just want our reputation restored."

He then looked at the jury and said, "I'll bet you've had days when your phone didn't work. I bet you called us and we came right out and fixed it."

The implication was that we should have just called the local repairman and had him come out and fix the problem. The jury took twenty minutes to decide for the phone company. Plus, even though they said they didn't want our money, the jury handed them $100 million for defamation. They handed them $40 million from me and $40 million from Roy Speer, personally, and $20 million from the company. Fortunately, we appealed the decision, and the entire suit was finally settled for a smaller sum, which was paid by our insurance company. But the impact on HSN was immeasurable. The trial cost us over $8 million in fees. It was a huge setback. It cost both sides millions of dollars in attorneys' fees and prevented us from doing what we do best—compete in the marketplace.

I'll always remember leaving the courtroom and having the newsmen stick microphones and cameras inches from my face and batter me with questions. I can understand why people get so mad at the paparazzi. But I ignored the reporters and refused to answer a question. Instead, we walked to our car, got in, and drove away, very dismayed.

You may recall the story I told earlier about the banker who said he learned how to make good decisions by making bad ones. It's true. My personal business plan for HSN projected sales of $5 billion by 1995. Yet, in 1998, HSN will do only a little more than it did a year after the lawsuit.

What did I learn? I learned that a lawsuit is like flipping a coin. You simply do not know the outcome. Since that's the case, I've learned to avoid litigation.

After that setback I restarted with a fresh realization that my game is commerce, and neither my ego nor a need to defend myself would put me on the sideline again.

Everyone and every business will encounter setbacks. We can't avoid them altogether. *But we can learn not to allow the same setbacks to hit us twice.* And that determination will enable us to restart in a way that will protect us from the second dream robber.

Don't misunderstand me. Dealing with dream robbers isn't as easy as a few simple steps. They may bruise your ego and tarnish your reputation. As long as you realize they have no power over you unless you give it to them, you'll be okay.

I always chuckle when I hear the story of the hard-hat employee whose accident report actually appeared on a company accident form. Bruised and bandaged, he related this experience:

When I got to the building I found that the hurricane had knocked off some bricks around the top. So I rigged up a beam with a pulley at the top of the building and hoisted up a couple of barrels full of bricks. When I had fixed the damaged area, there were a lot of bricks left over. Then I went to the bottom and began releasing the line. Unfortunately, the barrel of bricks was much heavier than I was—and before I knew what was happening the barrel started coming down, jerking me up.

I decided to hang on, since I was too far off the ground by then to jump, and halfway up I met the barrel of bricks coming down fast. I received a hard blow on my shoulder. I then continued to the top, banging my head against the beam and getting my fingers pinched and jammed in the pulley. When the barrel hit the ground hard, it burst its bottom, allowing the bricks to spill out.

I was now heavier than the barrel. So I started down again at high speed. Halfway down I met the barrel coming up fast and received severe injuries to my shins. When I hit the ground, I landed on the pile of spilled bricks, getting several painful cuts and deep bruises. At this point I must have lost my presence of mind, because I let go of my grip on the line. The barrel came down fast—giving me another blow on my head and putting me in the hospital.

I respectfully request sick leave.

No kidding! I tell that story because I think it illustrates how you may feel after suffering a beating from a major setback. In times like that, regroup, refocus, and most importantly, restart.

As you do this you'll discover the second dream robber can't walk away with your dream. But there is a third thief who will sneak into your life and try to slip away with your dream.

DREAM ROBBER THREE: ROADBLOCKS

We're all familiar with roadblocks. They're the barricades that block roads to keep travelers from moving forward. Usually they're put in place to protect people from danger. In business they're often just the litter of life. They're the bothersome problems that can slow things down or bring progress to a standstill. Roadblocks are usually the difficulties associated with the development of a new product or the implementation of a business plan. They may take the form of misguided or greedy people, seemingly unsolvable problems, or a personal response to betrayal or disappointment. Roadblocks can steal a dream by creating discouragement or physical exhaustion, or becoming a wasteful distraction.

Getting past a roadblock involves a combination of perseverance and mobility. It requires a willingness to hang in there, combined with the ability to get around the problem.

PERSONNEL PROBLEMS

Several years ago we bought a foreign TV station. The manager was a native and spoke the language. Because he had apparently done a good job, we decided to retain him as the manager after we closed on the deal.

Once a month, someone from the home office would fly to the station and monitor the station and evaluate the operation. It didn't take long for us to discover that the manager was probably embezzling funds and was being accused of sexual harrassment by a female employee. The manager was missing and the employee was threatening to sue us.

One morning I arrived at the office and saw the hallway cluttered with suitcases. Our three corporate lawyers were ready to fly off to find the manager, have him arrested, and protect us from the employee's lawsuit.

"Everybody get in the conference room," I said. "There are eight TV station acquisitions on which I've signed letters of intent to purchase. You're not all going. One lawyer can make the flight and settle the employee's claims. She deserves compensation. Pay her! Settle it quickly and fairly. We don't have time to chase the manager around. If we do that we won't be able to close on these new TV stations."

"You're not going to get that guy?" someone asked.

"Forget him. He's not worth it. We'll let the local authorities take care of him."

In a matter of days that problem had the power to become a roadblock barricading our progress on other important business. It's crucial for a leader to realize that sometimes the best way to deal with a roadblock is to go around it and move on. If we had become consumed with the situation we would undoubtedly have been prevented from seizing other opportunities.

SOMEONE MISSED IT!

Because we frequently utilize *stupid speed* in business, sometimes the roadblocks we encounter are created by our own shortcomings. For instance, when we were buying a television station in Honolulu, Hawaii, we moved quickly.

Once the deal was closed, construction began on the site on a hill overlooking Honolulu. The transmitter was shipped to the location, and heavy equipment was brought to the site.

Out of the blue I received an unexpected phone call from the landlord. "What's all of this equipment doing on the property?"

"We're building a television station," I said.

"Well, you don't have a lease!"

Holy cow! I said to myself. *How could this have happened?* We just agreed to pay $5 million for a station after it is built and we don't have a lease to build. I had someone race down the hall and grab the lawyers. A moment later three attorneys ran into my office."

"Where's the lease for the Hawaii station?" I asked.

"I-I-I-I-I'll have to check the files," one of them said as he raced out the door and down the hall. It didn't take him long to discover there was no finalized document.

The failure to sign that lease suddenly became a roadblock. What did we do? In a short time we solved the problem by agreeing to the landlord's terms and started construction.

These deals are complicated and the paperwork usually stands about a foot high. There is an asset-purchase agreement, an obligatory IRS appraisal, the tower lease, possibly a land lease or a land purchase, a survey, and a host of other elements that go into the deal.

Because we do so many television deals we have a system that enables us to go fast. It's like a doctor who performs nothing but open-heart surgery. He has a team of people who work with him. By developing a system they can perform more surgeries faster and better than other doctors who only perform one a year.

But occasionally our system encounters a roadblock. When it happens we try to quickly find a way around it.

HANG IN THERE

Oftentimes the key to getting past a roadblock is refusing to give up. Frequently, great ideas fail, not because they wouldn't eventually work, but because their champion surrendered. He got tired of dealing with the roadblocks and so he sat down, never to fight again.

A story is told about Thomas Edison, who invented, among other things, the electric lightbulb. A lightbulb works because a current is passed through a resistant material. When that material gets very hot it glows, creating light. The difficulty is that certain materials quickly burn up, even if kept in a vacuum where there is no oxygen. It took Thomas Edison a long time to discover this, and along the way he experimented with many different materials. One night he returned home and announced to his wife that he had just finished the ten thousandth experiment.

Now remember, not only did Edison have to cope with the repeated failures, but he also had to cope with those who criticized his idea and his experimental methods.

Anyway, when he arrived home and made that announcement, his wife asked, "Did it work?"

"Nope."

"Aren't you discouraged?" she asked.

"Discouraged? I now know ten thousand ways that won't work!"

Edison refused to allow one roadblock after another to discourage or dissuade him. He hung in there.

When a leader believes he has a dream that God has given him, he has an added reason to persevere. I'm convinced that getting through the eye of the needle involves defeating the dream robbers—the critics, the setbacks, and the roadblocks. When we do that we're able to bring to reality the vision God has given us. And when that occurs, God is pleased.

As I mentioned before, for most of my adult life my focus has been on business and the accumulation of wealth. But there is the second thread of life that is crucial. In the next section of the book we'll examine how we can get the spiritual thread through the eye of the needle.

7

HITTING BOTTOM

Without a doubt my all-time favorite movie is *Arthur*. I've actually watched it over two dozen times, and every time I watch the movie I'm touched. It's not the set or the costumes or the music or even the acting that draws me to the movie. It's the story.

Arthur is a middle-aged man who possessed great wealth—he's in line to inherit almost a billion dollars. Even though he had every possession a man could ever want—a mansion, limousine, butler, chef, personal assistant, and an unlimited expense account—Arthur was miserable.

One day, unexpectedly, Arthur fell in love. In fact, he fell so deeply in love that he was willing to turn his back on the family fortune in order to pursue the woman of his dreams. Ultimately, it was a person who filled the hole in Arthur's life. A hole that all of the money in the world couldn't fill.

I like the story of Arthur because, in many ways, it reflects my own life.

If anybody had looked at my life on Christmas morning 1986, he would have thought I had the world by the tail. And in many ways, I would have agreed. My vision and leadership had built HSN from a company that did $12 million in business in 1983 to a company that would eventually break the billion-dollar sales mark. As the president of a successful company I enjoyed all of the perks associated with that success.

In 1986 I was on the road about 260 days and visited countless countries. I traveled all over the world searching for products we could sell on HSN. In addition, I was traveling across the United States buying television stations. As a deal maker I was definitely in my element.

A FROG IN HOT WATER

Meanwhile, problems were brewing at home. I tried to call my wife every night, but I knew my absence was creating a gap in our relationship. The change occurred so slowly I wasn't aware how serious the problem had become.

My experience reminds me of the laboratory experiment that was performed on a frog. Initially, the frog was dropped into a vat of hot water. Without a moment's hesitation, the amphibian leaped out of the vat.

Next, the researcher placed the frog in a vat of cool water that was placed over a Bunsen burner. As the flame was slowly turned up, the frog never let out a croak or made any attempt to jump from the water. A short time later, it died in the boiling water. The frog died because the change in the temperature of the water was so gradual it never noticed.

In a sense, that's what happened to me. I could tell my marriage was slowly breaking down, but I didn't realize the extent of the problem until Christmas Day, 1986. I actually returned home on December 21 excited about the Christmas vacation I had planned for my entire family. We would all celebrate Christmas Day at home and then fly to Las Vegas. I hoped this time together would provide my wife and me with an opportunity to begin rebuilding our relationship.

I'll never forget the pile of presents. They filled much of the room and formed a pile as tall as a child. We all opened them from 9:00 A.M. until around 12:30. When we had finished opening the presents my wife said, "Bud, let's have some coffee out on the patio. I need to talk with you."

It was a beautiful sunny day. The warmth of the sun gave

no hint of what was about to happen. When my wife spoke, her words were like a bolt of lightning out of the blue Florida sky. "I'm leaving you," she said.

As those three words sank into my mind, I felt like somebody had grabbed my stomach and squeezed. And he wouldn't let go.

I knew things were bad. I had been gone. We hadn't spoken much, but I wanted to work on the relationship. I wanted to see what we could do to get closer. I didn't want her to leave. I wanted her to stay. I wanted her to go to Vegas with the rest of us.

But she left. On Christmas Day, she gathered up her presents and left me for another man.

SPIRITUAL BANKRUPTCY

My children had all gone back to their homes and I was in a house filled with presents—all alone. I had negotiated deals that had changed the way people shop—but I was alone. I had traveled the world—yet I was alone. I was rich—but I was alone. I had expensive cars and a luxurious house—but I was alone.

In that moment I realized my life had become totally empty. As that truth sank in, I placed my face in my hands and cried. For hours I wept.

I was absolutely and completely bankrupt. I was a millionaire, yet all of my success was worthless because I had lost my wife and wasn't close to my kids.

If I had possessed some sort of spiritual underpinnings, I might have withstood the blast. Or things might never have gotten so bad. But I didn't.

As a child growing up in Rochester, New York, my mother used to take me to church every week. I found the entire experience very tedious—to say the least. I remember how slowly time passed during those hours in Sunday school and church. While the pastor delivered his sermon I would crane my neck to see what the other kids were doing. I recall writing notes and gazing at the pictures in a book. What I don't recall is ever feeling like I connected with God.

WHAT IT MEANS TO BE BROKE

Once I left home I quit going to church and focused on the development of my entrepreneurial skills. And they needed a lot of development. In the early days they were as dull as an old razor. In fact, I had a hard time making enough money to keep my head above water. I can tell you from personal experience what it means to be broke. For me being broke is to be nine months behind on the house payment. It means to beg the bank to give me one more month to make a payment. To be broke means to have no food in the house, no gas in the car, no money in the bank, and no available credit on any credit card, and finally even emptying the kids' piggy banks. I've learned what it means to be broke.

During those times we lived in Sarasota, Florida. I remember going out to the deck at night and sitting under the stars. I was doing everything I could to bring in money to pay our bills, yet we were broke. I pleaded with God to give us money. Yes, I asked God for money.

GOD'S ANONYMOUS GIFT

Finally, things were so bad I got up one morning and planned on driving to McDonald's and applying for a job. I had to feed my family and saw no other alternative. Before getting in my car I collected the mail. As I opened an envelope a check slipped out and fell on the kitchen counter. I picked up the check and couldn't believe my eyes—it was written for $7,000.

The check was from an attorney's escrow account. I had sold something several years before, and an accountant had mistakenly left some of my money in the escrow account. For two years the money had been in the attorney's account drawing interest. When they did an audit of the account, the money showed up, so he sent me the check. Unfortunately, at that time I didn't connect with the one who anonymously orchestrated those events.

From that moment until this one, I have never been broke. That $7,000 literally turned things around, but that period of being broke also taught me the value of money. That doesn't mean I refuse to put my money at risk. Hey, I'm like a professional basketball player. Every time Michael Jordan puts the ball in the air he takes a risk. But experience has taught him that more balls will fall through the hoop than ricochet off the rim.

AM I SUCCESSFUL?

At a luncheon where I was speaking, the master of ceremonies introduced me as one of the most successful entrepreneurs in America. When I got up I changed the introduction of my speech and said, "Well, I'm going to let you decide whether or not I'm a great entrepreneur. I've started twenty-five businesses that I had to shut down because they didn't make enough money. I've had fifteen businesses that I sold for enough to make a little profit and cover the twenty-five unsuccessful efforts. And I've had two very big winners."

I then looked at the crowd and said, "Now you tell me, how successful am I?"

Over the long haul, I suppose I am. Today I have the fruit of two successful enterprises. But I also have forty other stories that nobody's ever written about. They included such things as a fast-food franchise, an art gallery, a marketing company, and an electronic sign company.

I realize that each of those unsuccessful endeavors provided me with a lesson that strengthened my entrepreneurial skills. They made me a better deal maker. I couldn't pull together the deals I orchestrate today without all of that experience. The problem was I focused my life entirely on business and pursued nothing but the game of commerce. I ignored God, my wife, and my children.

When my wife walked out I realized everything I had devoted my life to could not make me happy. I had enough money to go anywhere in the world. I could buy anything I wanted. But it was meaningless.

NEW YEAR'S EVE IN VEGAS

That Christmas I wanted to stay home, but my kids insisted I go with them to Vegas. They wanted to spend the time with me. They wanted to rebuild our relationship. That's amazing to me, since at that moment in time all they could see was a pitiful, spiritually bankrupt man—a father who was emotionally shattered.

After we arrived in Vegas we took a cab to Caesar's Palace. All of the lights and people and activity did nothing to ease my pain. On New Year's Eve, Buddy Hackett was performing, and the kids talked me into going with them. We had great seats near the stage, and Hackett was cracking one joke after another. Everyone in the audience was bent over with laughter. That is, everyone except me.

Partway through the show everyone received a party hat

and whistle. We were all going to usher in the New Year with loud noise and singing. I'll never forget staring at Buddy Hackett with tears streaming down my cheeks.

At 12:10 in the morning Hackett walked off the stage and I said, "Well, I'm going to bed."

"No, Dad. You can't go to bed," my kids said. "It's New Year's Eve, come on, you've gotta be with us!"

Finally, they all gathered around a slot machine and I sneaked off to my room. And what a room! A friend had provided me with a huge suite. It had to be one of the largest and most luxurious in Caesar's Palace. Of course, he had anticipated I would share it with my wife.

As I walked into that beautiful suite, it was probably the loneliest place in the world. I collapsed into a chair. Later, I sat on the end of the bed, but instead of sleeping, or even lying down, I just sat there and pondered worrisome, frightening, and unhappy thoughts.

THE TWILIGHT ZONE

My experience in Vegas reminded me of an East Coast gangster who unexpectedly visited a gambling establishment. His story is told on one of the old episodes of *The Twilight Zone*. Following his death, the ill-mannered hoodlum found himself in a beautiful penthouse in a high-rise casino. He soon realized things couldn't be better. In this new world he ruled like a king. Every time he gambled, he won. A beautiful woman laughed at his jokes and showered him with affection. He had everything he thought would satisfy.

Over time he found himself bored. Always winning and always getting what he wanted had eroded his pleasure. He craved a challenge and asked the gray-haired attendant if God hadn't sent him to heaven by mistake. The servant informed the man that God hadn't sent him to heaven. In that moment the gangster realized he was in hell.

While I wasn't in hell and hadn't been on a winning streak in the casino, I was surrounded with the trappings of success. Yet I was miserable.

THE THIRTY-FIFTH DRAWER

At 4:00 A.M. I glanced at my watch, looked around the room, and said to myself, *I bet you there's a Gideon Bible in here somewhere.*

Now remember, this was no small room, it was a suite. It actually had thirty-five drawers in the various chests and cabinets. I raced from one to the next, opening them and peering inside. I was in such a frantic hurry that I didn't close a single drawer. I opened them, looked inside, and moved on. Finally, in the thirty-fifth drawer, I found what I had been looking for.

I picked up the Bible and did the same thing millions of other people have done before me. I simply opened it and read what was on the page. Amazingly, the Bible opened to Job, Chapter 5. I read the story about how God could rescue Job from hardships and troubles and said, "Wow, that's my life."

I then turned to the front of the Bible and found the pages that directed me to the verses that would show me how to find peace with God. It was then that I discovered my sins had separated me from God. It wasn't that I was worse than the next guy, or as bad as I could be, but I knew I had thought, said, and done things that displeased God. And because of that I wasn't worthy to enter his presence. This truth didn't come as a big shock to me. I never thought of myself as a saint and I certainly wasn't religious.

I then turned to Romans 5:8, where I discovered that

Jesus Christ died on a cross to pay the debt of my sins. I have to admit that I had a few misconceptions about this. I guess I always saw Jesus as an example to follow or a teacher to learn from. While he is both of those, his death was far more. He died in my place and then rose from the dead. As a business-man I understood the concept of debt. And in that moment I realized someone else had paid the biggest debt of my life. Jesus had paid my spiritual debt with his life so I could go free.

Once I had grasped this truth, I was ready for the next one. The Gideon Bible then directed me to a verse that said all God wanted from me was faith. Part of my spiritual confusion had always centered on the belief that I had to do something to win God's acceptance. In Vegas I learned that all God wanted me to do was trust Jesus to forgive me and give me eternal life. God wanted me to exercise the same kind of faith I exercise every time I get on a plane and trust the pilot.

I FOUND PEACE

The moment I put my faith in Jesus Christ and trusted him to forgive me, an overwhelming peace came over me. I knew at that moment God loved me. I knew he was with me. I closed the Bible, put it on the bedstand, climbed into bed, and fell asleep.

A few hours later my kids came into my room and saw the thirty-five open drawers and panicked. "What happened?" they asked.

I smiled and told them, "I became a Christian last night."

The reality of my experience was validated by the immedi-ate changes that occurred in my life. For one thing, when we returned to Florida a couple of weeks had passed, and a friend from the office asked where I was going to church. Frankly, I hadn't thought about church yet. I was still basking in the peace I had found in Christ. That Sunday I went to church with my friend for the first time since my childhood. What's amazing is that I actually understood and appreciated what was going on.

A second thing that took place was I had an insatiable appetite to read and understand the Bible. I wanted to learn everything it said. In the next twenty days I read the entire Bible. I didn't get much out of it, but I read it because I wanted to know what it was about.

That desire led me to develop a relationship with the pastor at the church I first attended. He was gracious enough to explain to me the meaning of the Bible. I didn't try to figure it out myself. And I didn't buy a book that would explain it. I allowed a man who had devoted his life to studying and teaching the Bible to educate me. Dan Stuecher, the minister at Harborside Christian Church in Safety Harbor, Florida, provided me with friendship and love during the early years of my spiritual life. I am grateful that Dan was there and that he also provided me with well-thought-out answers to my questions and simple guidance through the various levels of spiritual growth.

It became clear to me after I returned to Florida that I should attempt to reconcile with my wife. In an effort to give the relationship another chance, the two of us decided to spend some time together and talk through our problems. Within a few days it was obvious that it wasn't going to work. She had found someone else and her heart was not in repairing our problems. It was then I knew there was nothing I could do to heal the marriage. It was broken beyond repair.

But my life wasn't broken beyond repair. I regret that I had to hit the bottom before I was willing to listen to God. But I'm thankful that when I did bottom out, He was waiting for me.

WHAT'S IN A NAME?

It's fascinating that it wasn't until after I became a follower of Christ that the meaning of my name was fleshed out in my experience. The first half of my last name, Pax, is Latin for "peace." Taken with the last three letters, my last name literally means "son of peace." As I mentioned earlier, the first emotion I experienced after trusting Christ was peace. My relationship with God had made me a son of peace.

In the fall of 1997, Dean Goodman, the president of our network, approached me and said, "Bud, I think we should call the new network PAX NET." I resisted the idea of putting my name in lights because I didn't want to be pretentious.

"Why do you want us to use that name?" I asked.

"Because it's catchy. People nowadays think in terms of the Internet. The term "net" is used with all sorts of products and services. But nobody says CBS Network or ABC Network. They just say CBS or ABC. But PAX NET flows. People won't say the PAX Network. They'll say PAX NET."

His reasoning made sense to the entire executive team, and so we went with the name PAX NET. And by then we had already purchased *Touched by an Angel*—a show that tells people about God's love. Once we chose the name it made sense to use the dove with an olive branch in its beak as our logo—and it fit like a glove. PAX NET will provide television viewers with programming that will allow them to discover true peace and that God loves them.

I'm concerned that too often religious people give the impression that a spiritual connection with God guarantees a problem-free life. It doesn't. But it does provide a place of shelter and comfort during life's greatest dangers and disappointments.

THE SHELTER OF GOD

On December 17, 1850, Captain Allen Gardiner and six companions landed at Patagonia on the southern tip of South America. They had made that long journey to bring the gospel to a people so primitive that evolutionist Charles Darwin said they existed "in a lower state . . . than in any other part of the world." Gardiner had prepared himself and his crew for the mission. He had made two previous visits to the region and knew that the natives were cannibals and that the land and weather were treacherous. His team included a doctor and a carpenter, and they brought with them a half year's supply of food and other goods. Gardiner's supporters in England had committed to send a relief ship of food after six months.

After his departure from England, Gardiner wrote, "Nothing can exceed the cheerful endurance and unanimity of the whole party. . . . I feel that the Lord is with us, and cannot doubt that He will own and bless the work which He permitted us to begin."

But as sometimes happens, something went wrong. A month after his departure, Gardiner's supporters still couldn't find a ship to carry the next six months' provisions to Patagonia. No one wanted to make such a dangerous journey. So, as the missionaries carried out their work on the cold tip of South America and as their supplies ran low, they scanned the horizon for the approaching ship. It never arrived. Those men faced a tough test. Alone in a hostile environment, without food or other supplies, hunger and death haunted them.

By the time a relief ship finally reached Patagonia in October 1851, the missionaries had all died of starvation. Clad in three suits, with wool stockings over his arms to ward off the numbing cold, Gardiner's emaciated body was found lying beside a boat.

What had that English missionary thought during those last horrifying days? Had the trial destroyed his faith? Were his dying days filled with nothing but pain? At one point, Gardiner wrote: "Poor and weak as we are, our boat is very Bethel [house of God] to our soul, for we feel and know that God is here. Asleep or awake, I am, beyond the power of expression, happy" (Stanley C. Baldwin, *Bruised But Not Broken*, Multnomah Press, 1985, pp. 20-21.)

Gardiner discovered that the shelter of God is available even in the midst of life's greatest difficulties. He found that the peace of God would always be with him.

While I never encountered anything like the physical hardships Gardiner underwent, I too found that when I hit bottom, God was there. I'm convinced that getting the spiritual thread through the eye of the needle begins when we meet God.

8

IT'S A PROCESS NOT A
DESTINATION

Television is a fantasyland. We enjoy watching it because it allows us to experience the rush of a car chase up and down the streets of San Francisco. It puts us in the control seat of Apollo 13. It allows us to experience the terror of swimming in water where killer sharks hunt. It enables us to vicariously embrace the most beautiful woman or handsome man. In the fantasyland of television anyone can become a powerful king, a superstar athlete or a master criminal.

Unfortunately, there are some television programs where the viewer is led to believe that fantasy is reality. I'm speaking of religious programming in which a televangelist describes the potential for a fantasy life that isn't linked to reality.

I've heard televangelists declare that people of faith never get sick. I've heard them promise financial prosperity to those who make a donation to their ministry. And I've heard them tell viewers that if they will simply believe, their compulsions, addictions, shortcomings, and relational issues will immediately be solved. It's as though faith activates a magic wand that God waves over the viewer's life and *presto!* their problems disappear. These shows lead the viewer to think faith activates spiritual maturity as instantly as a switch turns on a light.

Please don't misunderstand me. I'm not saying *all* religious programming presents fantasy as reality. But I am saying that all too often, behind the cloak of Christianity, fantasy is presented as reality and viewers are encouraged to believe it.

Perhaps you think my opinion is a bit extreme. I wish it were. But it isn't. Television is a place where techniques are used to improperly convince the viewer that fantasy is reality.

WHAT A DEAL!

I had an experience several years ago that illustrates what I mean. While I was at HSN a merchandise salesman called me and said, "I've got some beautiful ornate brass umbrella stands that are about three feet tall. I'll sell them to you for $15 apiece. They're solid brass, with beautiful arms that an umbrella rests on."

I was impressed with both the price and his description, so I asked him to send me one so I could examine it to determine the quality.

He FedExed me one of the umbrella stands and they were a good value. As I examined it more closely I saw something that made me laugh. Inside the base of the holder the manufacturer had printed in big letters: WEL COME.

The umbrellas were made in Taiwan and the original manufacturer didn't know how to spell the word "welcome." They spelled it "wel" followed by a space and then "come."

What did I do? I bought forty thousand, every one he had, for $5 each. I then found in a mail-order catalog the same umbrella stand that had a retail price of $67. I cut out the picture and went on television. I held up the picture from the catalog and said, "Ladies and gentlemen, look at that, $67 right out of the catalog. I'm going to give you a better deal than that. I'm going to sell you this brass umbrella stand for $30."

I then turned to the host and said, "Tell these people what they're getting." He took about three minutes to go over the fine details of the brass umbrella stand. I then rushed in front of the camera and said, "Oh, no! Stop the presentation!"

As the host stood speechless, I said, "Give me a camera. Bring the camera over here."

Turning to the host, I asked, "Bob, what idiot bought this? Look what we're stuck with." I then picked up the umbrella stand and tilted it toward the camera, allowing the viewer to see the unique spelling of "welcome."

"How stupid is this? Whoever made this doesn't even know how to spell the word 'welcome.' They've spelled it 'WEL COME.' We can't sell this. Nobody will pay $30. Let's see if we can get rid of this mistake for $10."

In ten minutes we sold all forty thousand umbrella holders.

Did the people get a good deal? Yes, they got a fair deal. But the entire presentation was staged. It was a fantasy. That's what television is all about. It's a fantasy. As long as the viewer knows that, it's okay. But when they actually believe the fantasy, their misplaced faith can lead to severe disillusionment.

That's what happens when the televangelist *only* tells stories of people who recovered from a severe disease, or gave money to a ministry and got rich, or prayed and a rebellious child came home. It's what happens when stories are *only* told by people who became Christians and instantly were delivered from addictions, recovered from illness, and experienced healing of relational wounds. The impression is that *spiritual* Christians are automatically mature—regardless of their background. The message is that *spiritual* Christians don't suffer—regardless of their health history, job, or relationship circumstances.

Many people want to believe such an illusion is reality. Just like viewers wanted to believe I discounted those umbrella holders from $30 to $10 because of a misspelled word in the base of the holder.

God's love doesn't offer a *quick* fix for human struggles.

He does provide us with a fix. But it isn't a quick one. He invites us into a relationship with himself that grows over a lifetime. That growth is the rock that holds us up so we can endure hardship. Ultimately, the struggles God allows us to encounter are designed to strengthen our characters. Spiritual maturity isn't a destination someone arrives at. It's a process. And the process is where life is lived.

I'm convinced threading the needle involves my willingness to open myself to God, so the process will proceed in a way that pleases him. How can we do that? Obviously there is no magic formula. But I've identified three principles that have proven helpful to me.

First: I must remain committed to truth.

Those of us who want to thread the needle with our spiritual lives would be wise to commit ourselves to truth. After reading my story about the umbrella stand you may raise an eyebrow and say, "So truth is important to you? Really? Well, why didn't you remember that when you were staging the sales pitch for the umbrella stands?"

Hey, I've done a lot of things that I look back on with either regret or discomfort. I used that story to illustrate the fact that people in television, and especially televangelists, stage their shows so that fantasy looks like reality. Once I accepted Jesus Christ, I discovered a number of things in my life where change was needed. Frankly, I wouldn't be comfortable staging that kind of a sales pitch today.

That's what it means to be in process. We start where we are and move forward, seeking each day to become more truthful than we were the day before. Instead of winning a business deal or impressing a friend with tricks, we speak the truth and let the chips fall where they may.

DIG UP THE STONES

When I was growing up my parents had a cottage with a large yard. Every winter the frigid weather and frost would push stones up to the surface of the ground. In the late spring, before we could mow the lawn, we would have to walk through the yard and dig up the stones and throw them away. Occasionally, I would have to dig up a large stone and replace the grass where it had been removed.

I realize that in the process of spiritual growth problems will surface in my life, things that are displeasing to God and that need to be addressed and removed. Periodically, those I think have been removed will appear in another form. None of us will ever reach a point in our lives where we can smile and say, "I've arrived."

A story is told about four people—a Boy Scout, a pastor, a computer scientist, and a doctor—who were the only passengers on a commercial flight from New York to San Francisco. After the plane had attained cruising altitude, the pilot stepped out of the cockpit and informed the passengers that the engines had failed and the plane was going down. Unfortunately, they only had enough parachutes for the flight crew and three passengers. One of the passengers would have to go down with the plane.

A moment later, the flight crew donned their parachutes and leaped from the crippled plane. The four passengers looked at each other, uncertain what to say. All of a sudden, the doctor leaped to his feet, put on a parachute, and said, "I'm the only man alive who knows how to perform a life-saving brain operation." He then jumped from the plane.

The scientist quickly put on a parachute and said, "I'm the most brilliant scientist in the world. For the sake of humanity, I must live," and he too leaped from the plane.

The pastor looked at the Boy Scout and said, "Son, you have your entire life to live, please take the remaining parachute."

The Boy Scout tossed a parachute into the pastor's lap and said, "Put on the parachute, Reverend. The smartest man in the world just leaped out of the plane wearing my backpack."

I think that story illustrates what can happen to any of us when we believe we've attained some higher level of spiritual insight. Such thinking sets us up for a big fall. This is true in the area of honesty. We need to make an effort to continually examine our lives to make sure we're standing by our commitment to truth.

TRUTH NOT TRICKS

There's always the temptation to rely on tricks rather than truthfulness, especially with television. When a ministry needs huge amounts of money to stay on the air, the televangelist might promise, "If you'll send money, we'll give you this flask of healing oil that will take away the pain of your arthritis—if you'll apply it and believe God will heal you." Such a promise lets the televangelist off the hook if the person's symptoms don't improve. He can always say the person who applied the oil didn't exercise enough faith.

Is that approach honest. No! It's built around tricks rather than truth. Can God heal? Of course he can. Will God heal everyone who applies oil to an arthritic joint and exercises faith in him? No, he will not.

Miraculous healing is not the normal avenue God utilizes in dealing with us. I wish it were. I have a daughter whom I love dearly and who suffers from lupus. I've prayed on hundreds of occasions for her healing. I have recently committed myself to pray every day for the next year. While God could heal her, he has not chosen to do so at this writing.

Instead, he allows scientists to investigate the laws of nature so they can discover the cause of a disease. Once they uncover the cause they may then be able to develop a cure. Such an approach is based on the reliability of the natural laws of the universe. It is based on the belief that God heals people when scientists understand the truth about why they are sick and how the illness can be reversed. In either case, since God put the laws of nature in place, the cure comes from him. Like truth, these laws are reliable. When understood and utilized for our benefit, they result in great good.

We need to rely on truth, not tricks, to achieve our ends. And we need to guard ourselves from those who use tricks to impress us. As we seek truth, we'll need to remember a second principle that will help the process of our spiritual growth.

Two: I will try to trust in God because I know he cares for me and doesn't make mistakes.

If we believe God doesn't make mistakes, then it makes sense we should trust him. The more we trust God, the more we will try to obey him. Ultimately, the direction he gives us is for our best interest. He even orchestrates circumstances for our own good.

The day I received the $7,000 check in the mail, God was working behind the scenes. The day the retailer paid me with 112 can openers, God was backstage calling the shots. The fact that we were able to buy all those television stations prior to a ruling on *must carry* shows God working in the shadows.

TOUGH CHOICES

Sometimes the demands God makes on our lives are tough. In the opening chapter I mentioned the story of the rich young ruler. The man viewed himself as having arrived spiritually. Motivated by love, Jesus challenged him to do the one thing that would expose the man to his true character. Had the man been willing to give his earthly treasure to the poor, he would have become the receptacle of God's riches here on earth. No material treasure could match that.

In a moment the man was forced to make a decision between obeying or disobeying the command of Jesus. Sadly, the man's possessions were more important to him than the privilege of a relationship with God. He had become insepara-bly linked to his wealth and couldn't imagine life without it.

In my travels I've seen parts of the world where camels are still used as a mode of transportation. I suspect that in ancient Israel there was no animal larger than a camel and no hole smaller than the eye of a needle. Those who trust in their riches to buy them a ticket into the kingdom of God will never make it.

I've been told that Jesus wasn't just talking about how the man could get into heaven. The kingdom of God referred to God's rule over everything, his dominion over our possession, relationships, responsibilities—all of our life. Ultimately, all we have belongs to God. The issue Jesus confronted the man with involved his willingness to acknowledge God's authority over his life. Jesus wanted to know if the man was willing to place obedience to Him over everything else in life.

HELP! I'M STUCK

All too often we hang on to things that prevent us from obey-ing God. A story is told of a young boy who ran to his mother screaming, "I've caught my hand in the vase. It won't come out!"

His mother calmed the boy and tried to free his hand. She pulled on the vase, but that didn't work. She shot liquid soap over his hand, and that didn't work either. Eventually, she gave up and told her son they would have to wait until his dad got home. "He'll be able to get your hand out," she assured the distraught boy.

The boy's mother knew they could break the vase if they had to. But she didn't want to do that because it was a valuable heirloom that had been in her family for five generations. When her husband finally walked in the front door a crying boy and frantic mother met him there. Unfortunately, he had no better luck than his wife. While attempting to calm the boy, he took a small hammer and lightly tapped on the body of the priceless vase. Instantly, the porcelain cracked and fell apart, revealing the boy's clenched fist.

"Son, have you been clutching your fist the entire time we were trying to get your hand out of the vase?" his father asked.

With tears streaming down his cheeks, the child nodded his head up and down.

"But why?"

"Because I didn't want to let go of my quarter," the boy said as he opened his hand, revealing a shiny quarter.

That boy had just sacrificed a priceless heirloom because he wouldn't let go of a quarter. The rich young man Jesus spoke with sacrificed much more than a vase because he wouldn't let go of his money.

DEFINING MOMENTS

I've discovered that obedience to God involves defining moments when I sense God wants me to do something. It may be a reminder that he wants me to clean up my language—this is an area that seems to go away and then suddenly returns to haunt me. It may be a reminder that I need to do a better job controlling my temper, which I have done. Or it may be something like developing a television network that provides the public with family-oriented programming.

Whenever the defining moment occurs, a part of me resists obeying God. I want to hold on to whatever it is God is urging me to change or hand over to him. At those times I'm trying to remember that it is only by the grace of God that the camel gets through the eye of the needle. I can only obey him as I ask for his grace and strength to help me make decisions that please him.

One thing that makes obeying God so hard is the belief that if I obey him, I could lose my quarter. I could end up on the losing side of the deal. That's where I have to believe that God doesn't make mistakes. God will never ask me to do something unless it's for my ultimate good.

I'm reminded of the frustration of putting together a large puzzle. Imagine how hard it would be without the picture on the box top. None of the pieces would make any sense. Of course, nobody selects a puzzle by dumping out the pieces on a table and examining them. We choose a puzzle because we like the picture on the box.

In life we only have the pieces of the puzzle. We've never even seen the big picture. God holds it. Our job is to obey God by placing the pieces of the puzzle where he commands. To do that we must believe that he knows how everything will fit together.

Learning to obey God is a lifelong process. For me it began in a suite in Las Vegas when I obeyed God by trusting Jesus to forgive me. Since then my spiritual growth has been a series of three steps forward and two steps back.

The issue of obedience to God rests on our ability to choose. That brings me to the third principle I want to consider.

Three: Because God allows us to make our own choices, we need to make choices that stimulate our spiritual growth.

Sometimes the press communicates the idea that there are religious elements in our country that would like to censor what is on television. They give the impression these people think everyone should believe as they do. And if everyone doesn't believe as they do, he or she should at least share their moral and social values.

I don't think it's my job to tell others what they should believe. Nor is it my role to dictate the moral or social values of our country. God does not impose himself on people. He presents them with the truth and allows them the freedom to choose what they want to do.

Jesus didn't impose his will on the rich young ruler. He extended a challenge and then let the man choose which he wanted—his money or God. Furthermore, when the man turned away, Jesus didn't chase him down and soften the challenge. The command was clear. And so was the man's choice.

GOD'S COMMITMENT TO OUR FREE WILL

I'm impressed that Jesus didn't resort to a "sign" or "trick" to convince the rich young man to follow him. Think about it. As Jesus, God in human form stood before that man. Jesus could have picked up a stone and turned it to gold. He could have said to the man, "You don't need to trust in your own entrepreneurial skills or your bank account. Follow me and I'll take care of you."

Jesus' commitment to that man's free will was so complete that he refused to use a miracle to manipulate him. Why? Because he wanted love to summon the man. Not a miracle.

Jesus wanted the man to let go of his money because he loved God. Jesus knew only love could conquer the human heart.

One of the dangers of television is that it provides some people with opportunities to stage "miracles" that attract people to Jesus. There are exceptions, of course. Billy Graham, James Dobson, James Robison, James Kennedy, Charles Stanley, Ben Haden, and others all use television in an honorable way. But all too often a lot of television preachers have forgotten the motto that says, "My utmost for *His* highest." If they remember, then their shows would have high ratings.

The Jesus some of them present is like an ancient version of David Copperfield. They do miracles over television to "wow" the audience. Is their audience drawn to Jesus by love? I'm not so sure. It seems to me that they're attracted to the illusion they think will turn their rocks into gold, someone who will take away their hurts and replace them with health *if only* they'll send in a donation.

Sure, Jesus performed miracles. But not to wow the crowd so they would follow him. Instead, he invited people to a relationship with himself. And he wanted them to be drawn by love.

Our desire at PAX NET is to provide people with the opportunity to choose programs that will reinforce family values. I do not believe television is capable of developing a person spiritually. We can only plant the seed of faith through positive programming that communicates God's love and presence. A person needs Bible study, prayer, and fellowship in order to grow spiritually. The Bible makes it quite clear where growth occurs . . . the Church.

Of course, I know there are exceptions. Sometimes the elderly or bedridden can't physically go to a place of worship. Television allows them to view a service. But they too need Bible study, prayer, and spiritually challenging friends.

MAKING A DIFFERENCE

That realization may cause someone to ask, "Can PAX NET make a difference?" Of course we can! But I realize we're not here to replace the church. Our job is to plant a seed that will prompt people to go find a place of ministry where they can grow. A place where they can hear about and respond to the love of God. A church they can join.

Whenever someone indicates our network won't make any lasting difference, I'm reminded of the story of a man who was walking down a deserted beach in South America. As he walked, he noticed a local native in the distance who kept bending over, picking up something, and tossing it into the water.

What's he doing? the man said to himself.

In a few minutes they were close enough so that he could see the man was throwing starfish back into the water. When the two were side by side, the onlooker asked, "Are you having fun?"

"I'm throwing these starfish back into the ocean. It's low tide and all of these starfish have been washed up onto the shore. If I don't throw them back into the sea, they'll die on the beach."

"I understand. But there must be thousands of starfish on this beach. You can't possibly get to all of them. There are simply too many. And don't you realize this is probably happening on hundreds of beaches all up and down this coast? Can't you see that you can't possibly make a difference?"

The local man smiled, bent down, and picked up another starfish, and as he threw it back into the ocean, he replied, "Made a difference to that one."

We want to be a part of the process of spiritual growth in the lives of Americans. And each time we help a family move closer to God, we'll know we've made a difference.

9
DISCERNING GOD'S WILL

It never ceases to amaze me that people will actually call a 900 number so they can talk to a "professional psychic." Twenty-four hours a day the commercials run on television. Twenty-four hours a day the calls pour in to the operators. Some of the commercials are only thirty-second spots, and others are half-hour infomercials.

"Our psychics are different from the others," the pitch goes. "They're trained. They can tell you if your future holds romance, wealth, or an exciting vacation."

Once the initial pitch has been made, the testimonials begin. "I couldn't believe it," the beautiful coed says. "My psychic said I would meet a tall, handsome, dark-haired man. One week later I met John."

The fantasy these so-called "psychics" perpetuate is that they can actually read the future. If even one of those phonies could read the future, people would eagerly pay them $10,000 for tomorrow's stock prices. But evidently there are enough believers out there so that some of these companies reap a handsome profit.

ALICE IN WONDERLAND

People who seek guidance from psychics remind me of a scene from *Alice in Wonderland.* Alice had just arrived at a junction in the road that led in different direction. Turning to the Cheshire Cat, she asked for advice.

"Cheshire-Puss . . . Would you tell me, please, which way I ought to go from here?"

"That depends a good deal on where you want to get to," said the Cat.

"I don't much care where," said Alice.

"Then it doesn't matter which way you go," said the Cat.

That grinning feline spoke words of truth. If we don't know where we want to go, then any road will take us there. I suppose many people turn to psychics because they don't really know where they want to go. If that's the case, then it also makes sense that they don't care who gives them directions.

I realize not everyone turns to psychics, horoscopes, or palm readers for direction. Most people share my level of disregard for such guidance and prefer to trust in their own judgment and faith to guide their decisions.

A BETTER WAY

I'm convinced there is a better way, a way that utilizes a person's judgment and instincts but also taps into God's wisdom. It's not as simple as calling a 900 number. And it's not as specific as the guidance you would receive from a road map. But it can connect you with God and enable you to discern the direction he wants your life to take. I'm fortunate that my pastor, Dan Stuecher, early in my Christian experience gave me five principles aimed at helping me make good decisions—decisions that would enable me to thread the needle by relying on God's grace.

If you think I'm going to share with you how you can hear the voice of God, I'm afraid you'll be disappointed. I've never heard God speak to me. At least not in an audible voice. It's never happened. These principles aren't a magic formula. They're great guidelines aimed at helping a person discover what God wants him or her to do in a specific situation. If you have an important decision to make and you would like to discern God's will, I think these will help you. I know they've helped me.

As you read on, keep the following in mind. We each have a conscience. Think about yours. Basically, your conscience works by telling you what not to do. We say we have a *guilty conscience*. This is because we did something we shouldn't have done. At the same place in your mind where you hear your conscience tell you what not to do, you can develop the positive side of your conscience to hear what you should do. It will become a *knowing* and will stand up before the following principles.

Principle One: Ask yourself if the course of action you are considering complies with biblical principles.

The basic thrust of this principle is that God never wants me to do something that will violate biblical principles. If I'm praying for guidance as to whether or not I should twist the truth or weasel out of a contract or manipulate circumstances to get what I want, I'm wasting my time. The Bible tells me to be honest. That means God will never direct me to do something that compromises his principles.

Before I became a Christian I knew very little about the Bible. Yet, as I read through it, I discovered I could understand its message and identify important principles. As my faith grew, I could reread a passage and learn new principles. That is the miracle of the Bible. It is written in such a way that you can learn more every time you read it. This alone has convinced me of the fact that the Bible is the work of God. Regardless of how well you may know the Bible, you too will find that by searching its pages you'll constantly discover new principles that will guide your decision making.

For instance, a key biblical teaching is that we should not be "unequally yoked" in our relationship (II Corinthians 6:14). The imagery Paul used spoke of two oxen pulling a wagon or plow. Each ox would have a yoke that hung on its shoulders. The wagon or plow would be attached to the yoke. If the oxen were of different sizes, then the larger animal would bear most of the weight. Not only would the stronger ox wear out faster, but a farmer would have trouble plowing a straight furrow.

While the biblical passage speaks about the importance of people sharing spiritual beliefs, it addresses a broader principle: "Don't go into business with someone who doesn't share your vision and values."

Several years ago I had just finished giving a speech to an audience of businessmen when a man approached me, introduced himself, and said, "I have a plumbing business that is doing well, but I'm not sure I should stay in business with my partner."

"Why not?" I asked.

"Our business is making a good profit and I want to put some of the money into the community by doing things like sponsoring Little League baseball teams. He wants us to keep all of the money."

After giving that example he said, "Sponsoring baseball teams isn't the issue. It's just that the current problem demonstrates the fact that we have vastly different values and it causes ongoing tension in our relationship."

As the conversation ended he told me he had decided to begin the process of buying out his partner. Why had he made that decision? Because he knew that their partnership violated the biblical principle that we're not to be in business with people who do not share our vision and values.

It's also a good idea to apply this principle to personal decisions. It didn't take me long after my divorce to realize I didn't like the single life. After I became a Christian I discovered I should marry only someone who shared my faith and values. When I went out for the first time with someone I asked her a single question: "What do you think of Jesus Christ?"

Not until I met Marla did I hear the right answer.

Marla said, "I've known him all my life. What would you like to know?"

I replied, "I'd like to know what you are doing Friday night."

That answer told me our relationship could move to the next step. It culminated in a marriage so beautiful, so like a storybook, I thank God every day for her and what He has given me.

Discovering God's will begins by discerning whether or not a course of action complies with the biblical principles. That means if I have a decision to make I need to study the Bible to see what principles apply to my situation. If a course of action violates those principles, then I need to abandon it. If it complies, then I need to look at the next principle.

Principle Two: If he's behind something, God will open doors so I won't have to knock them down.

The idea of God opening doors for me doesn't imply I can sit back in a lounge chair and wait for God to do all the work. I need to seize strategic opportunities and move forward with them. But if I meet one closed door after another, which I have to knock down to get through, then God's probably not in the course of action.

IS THAT DOOR CLOSED?

It's easy to think this idea is abstract and you could never know for sure if God is opening the door or you're knocking it down. I guarantee you, the difference becomes very clear.

When we first formed the *Worship* TV program, our initial intention was to air it on every Christian television station in the United States. The idea certainly passed the first test—there were a lot of biblical principles to support our concept for the program. But it took about a year to realize continuing in this direction would require knocking down some hefty doors.

For instance, to fund the program we initially experimented with a 900-number phone prayer line. At that time phone sex companies and psychic counselors were aggressively advertising their 900 numbers. The American public associated 900 numbers with phone sex and psychics. We gave up the idea of using a 900 number after a few weeks because we were banging on doors that God would immediately close.

While *Worship's* viewers do spontaneously tithe to the ministry, the monthly expenses outstripped the income by a ratio of five to one. If God had wanted us to continue to air the show over Christian TV stations, either the financial results would have been better because of unsolicited gifts, or we would have to begin asking for donations. Since we knew God did not want us to ask viewers for money, to continue down that path would have meant knocking down some financial doors that were locked shut.

WALKING THROUGH OPEN DOORS

In contrast to that was our 1997 purchase of the television station in New York. The station we wanted to buy was WNYC-

TV, and it was owned and operated by the city of New York. Because the city didn't really know how to run a station or chose to run the station without a profit, they aired one low-quality program after another.

Faced with intense financial needs, New York City decided to sell the station. Since they had never sold a TV station, they hired an investment banker and determined to hold an auction. In the first round we bid $85 million and made it to the next round. Before the second round, which would occur a few days later, our team met to brainstorm regarding our next bid. We figured if we bid $85 million, somebody else would bid $100 million. So we thought we would bid $101 million.

"No, we can't do that," someone said. "A competitor might round out their bid at $105 million."

That made sense, so we decided to bid $106 million. And we lost!

To our surprise the winning bid was not $107 million. It was $207 million. We weren't sure what had happened. Did ITT and Dow Jones think that our final bid was $206 million so they would beat it by one million? If so, they topped our bid by $101 million. It seems as though their information was off by $100 million.

At the time it seemed the door to that station was closed. And it was. But another door opened a year later, when a large company attempted a hostile takeover of ITT. In reaction to the takeover, ITT started selling off non-core business properties. I read a story about what was happening and so I set up a meeting in New York City with officers of ITT.

Those two companies, ITT and Dow Jones, had poured millions into the station. According to what I had read, they had installed $30 million worth of TV equipment and had sustained $20 million in losses. I knew exactly what they had paid for it and how much they had invested. When we met, I had done my homework.

"Do you want to get the $257 million out of it that you've put into it?" I asked.

"That's what we want," they said.

"Sold!" I said without a moment's hesitation.

So far it seemed the doors were wide open for a quick negotiation.

They then had second thoughts. "Well, we probably ought to conduct an auction."

"If you're going to put it up for auction, I'm out of here," I said before they could continue. "And I'm not coming back. You want my $257 million, you take it today. Otherwise, say-onara, my friend, I'm outa here. You want to hire an investment banker, be my guest. But I won't be involved."

"Well, we have a partner, Dow Jones," they said.

At that time, I knew another door had been opened—ITT would sell their share if Dow Jones was willing to sell.

"You have a partner, good. Pick up the phone and set up an appointment."

They picked up the phone and called Peter Skinner over at Dow Jones. After our conversation I went to Skinner's office.

"You guys want to sell today for $257 million?" I asked. "I'll pay you right now, but I'm not negotiating a dime. That's what you've got in it and that's what I'll pay for it."

"I have to talk to our partners over at ITT," he said.

"I just came from there," I told him. "Call them on the phone right now while I'm here."

Fifteen minutes later he sent me back to ITT. I had been there only a few minutes when the president of ITT walked into the office with an entourage of people and said, "You've got a deal."

Another door had opened.

I asked one of the men with him, "Are you his lawyer."

"Yes, I am."

"You're doing the paperwork?" I continued.

"That's right."

I called John Feore, our FCC lawyer in Washington, D.C., and had him on a plane the next day so they could take care of the details. Days later we signed the papers, and I transferred $25 million to them as a deposit.

Door after door had opened. But that's not the end of the story. We now had a TV station in New York, but we needed programming so it could make money. *Dow Jones Business News* had been on the station. The moment they left TV, another door opened, when their biggest competitor, *Bloomberg Financial News*, bought their twelve-hour time slot. We sold the rest of the time to infomercials and put *Worship* on overnight. The cash flow for the first year would be over $24 million. Not bad!

But one more door had to open. We had to come up with the rest of the money to pay for the station. That happened when we sold the radio group for $633 million, which allowed us to pay for the New York station and a dozen or so more TV stations.

I've told that story because it illustrates how quickly doors can open when a course of action is in keeping with God's will. However, discerning God's will involves more than walking through a series of open doors. There is a third principle that must be examined.

Principle Three: If God favors a course of action it will be logical and make good common sense, so I won't need to rationalize what I'm doing.

God created us with the capacity to reason. That ability enables us to evaluate the pros and cons of a specific situation.

I've had scores of people tell me they felt God was directing them to take a course of action that others saw as foolhardy. Even though they were urged to reconsider, they moved forward. Later, when the venture failed, they blamed God for directing them down such an illogical path.

SIZE UP THE SITUATION

God doesn't direct us to abandon our common sense. We're to be like the cowboy who walked out of a saloon and discovered somebody had painted his horse's tail red. As bystanders doubled over with laughter he burned with rage. "Who painted my horse's tail red?"

"Some guy over there in the hardware store," a boy said, pointing across the street. The man stormed over to the hardware store, muttering to himself, "I'll tear him limb from limb."

He slammed open the door to the store. "Who painted my horse's tail red?" he spat out, clenching his fists at his side.

An enormous six-foot-seven-inch blacksmith stepped out from behind a roll of barbed wire. The man looked like he had been chiseled out of granite. "I did," he growled. "Why?'

The cowboy quickly sized up the blacksmith and said, "Looks to me like the first coat is dry and ready for a second one. Did you want to paint it yourself or should I?"

I'm not sure how spiritual his enlightenment was, but it made sense. That cowboy didn't need to pray in order to figure out the best course of action. Occasionally, God may direct us to take risks. But every risk should be evaluated and its likelihood of success determined. If I have to abandon my common sense to pursue a course of action, I'll assume that course of action isn't from God.

Throughout the process of discerning the will of God I try to follow the fourth principle.

Principle Four: Take time to pray before rushing into something.

While I believe in *stupid speed,* I don't rush forward until I have a sense God is in something.

TALKING WITH GOD

Prayer puts me in touch with God. It enables me to sense his direction. As I mentioned earlier, I've never heard God's voice. He's never spoken to me with a sign. I realize such a confession may cause some people to think that I'm not in touch with God at all. I believe you will get a *knowing*. You can develop, just like your conscience, the ability to hear the still small voice of God.

People who use televangelists for their spiritual standard may view me as less than spiritual. I know that on numerous occasions I've heard televangelists say, "God spoke to me." The impression I get listening to them is that they regularly carry on a two-way *audible* conversation with God. I've never had such a conversation. Frankly, I don't believe they have either.

Prayer for me is primarily an act of worship. It's the way I give thanks to God for his goodness and tell him of my love. Throughout the day I try to periodically pause just to express my adoration to God.

In the process of making a decision I scan my internal sensors to see if I detect an awareness that God is urging me forward or telling me to pull back. Early on in my Christian experience I was out on my boat one night, several miles from shore, pleading with God for a sign. I asked him for something to show me what I should do. Just as I finished praying I saw a beautiful meteor streak across the southern sky.

Believing I had my sign, I moved forward with the plan. When things blew up in my face I asked my pastor what had happened.

"Bud," he said, "God doesn't send messages to us with shooting stars. Forget that."

It took me a while to realize God speaks to us through the Bible and through an internal sensing of what he wants. Our conscience tells us what *not* to do. But God's Spirit prompts us concerning what we *should* do. It is a *knowing*.

SENSING GOD'S MESSAGE

For instance, when the cable industry took *must carry* all the way to the Supreme Court to have it overturned, I had plenty to worry about. We were buying our first three TV stations at that time. If the cable companies weren't forced by the court to carry our TV programs, our stations would lose audiences and value. I vividly remember talking the matter over with God, and I sensed him telling me, "Don't worry about *must carry*." It was not an audible voice. It was a sensing in my heart, a *knowing*, that was emblazoned on my spirit.

God didn't say, "Bud, *must carry* will be upheld by the Supreme Court." I couldn't know what would happen in the future. Such an idea isn't biblical. I sensed God didn't want me to worry about *must carry*. It began as a *knowing* in my spirit that became very firm—"Don't worry about *must carry*." So I didn't. During this period from the summer of '94 until April of '97, we expressed our belief in God's message of "Don't worry" by buying fifty more stations.

Discerning God's will involves talking to God about the decision and then quietly waiting to see if God gives a sense of what he wants. As you do this, you'll also want to be reviewing the fifth principle. It's the one that's easy to rush past, especially if the decision is one you favor and those close to you may oppose. That's what makes the final principle so important.

Principle Five: God wants me to discuss the decision with my Christian friends and other important people in my life.

The tendency for most people is to ask advice only from individuals who will tell them what they want to hear. I've found it helpful to seek counsel from friends and deeply rooted Christians who share my moral and spiritual values. If I'm in the process of making a decision that violates the teachings of the Bible or one that lacks common sense, I want to know before the decision is acted on. Solomon noted the importance of obtaining sound advice when he said, "Plans fail for lack of counsel, but with many advisors they succeed" (Proverbs 15:22).

Of course there are plenty of examples of people who made wrong choices and recovered from them. Moses is a classic example. As a member of Egyptian royalty he was destined for political greatness inside the Egyptian court. But because of his love for the Jewish people, his people, he killed an Egyptian he saw beating a Hebrew man. In an effort to hide his crime, Moses buried the man's body in the sand. Later, when his act was discovered, Moses fled to the wilderness, where he lived for forty years.

That impulsive decision cost Moses dearly. But he recovered and became the man who led the Hebrew people out of Egypt and into freedom. We all make mistakes. But we can also recover from those mistakes. Our goal should be to make decisions that lead to success—decisions God favors, those that will enable us to avoid costly mistakes.

The process of discerning God's will is something we have

to work on throughout our lives. It's a process that requires discipline. We will improve with practice, but it's a process we will never completely master. Why? Because we're human. We're sinners, and we often want what *we* want, not what God wants.

However, it's more than just reviewing five principles. Ultimately, finding and carrying out God's will requires faith. Once we sense what we're supposed to do, we need to believe that God's guidance can be trusted. In Proverbs 3:5–6 we're told, "Trust in the Lord with all your heart and lean not on your own understanding; in all your ways acknowledge him, and he will make your paths straight."

DESERT PETE

In a sense, we're to be like the man who found a letter written by Desert Pete.

I've heard it was discovered many years ago in a tin tied to an old pump on a remote desert trail.

Dear Friend,

The pump is all right as of June 1932. I put a new sucker washer into it and it ought to last five years. But the washer dries out and the pump has to be primed. Under the white rock I buried a bottle of water, out of the sun and corked up. There's enough water in it to prime the pump, but not if you drink some first. Pour about one fourth and let her soak to wet the leather. Then pour in the rest medium fast and pump like crazy. You'll get water. The well has never run dry. Have faith. When you get watered up, fill the bottle and put it back as you found it for the next fellar.

Desert Pete

Like the man who found that note, we need to follow the instructions we receive from God and have faith. If we'll do that, he'll never let us down. And we'll end up making decisions that please him and lead to success.

10
CAPITALIZING THE KINGDOM

In 1923, seven of the world's most successful businessmen gathered in a posh meeting room at the Edgewater Hotel in Chicago. The stated purpose of their meeting: *How to make more money.*

Collectively, these tycoons controlled more wealth than there was in the United States Treasury at the time, and for years newspapers and magazines printed their success stories and urged the youth of our nation to follow in their footsteps. However, just twenty-eight years later the last of the seven men had died and their obituaries told a different story.

Charles Schwab, president of the largest independent steel company of the day, lived on borrowed money the last five years of his life and died penniless.

Arthur Cutten, one of the greatest wheat speculators of our century, escaped overseas and died insolvent.

Richard Whitney, president of the New York Stock Exchange, spent time at Sing Sing.

Albert Fall, former U.S. Senator and Secretary of the Interior under Warren Harding, was pardoned from prison so he could die at home.

Jesse Livermore, one of the most famous speculators on Wall Street . . . suicide.

Leon Fraser, president of the Bank of International Settlement . . . suicide.

Ivar Kreuger, head of one the world's greatest monopolies . . . suicide.

All of them had learned how to make money, but none of them had learned how to live.

Too many people spell success M.O.N.E.Y. Like the aforementioned, they spend so much of their lives trying to be successful through the acquisition of money, or what money brings, they never learn how to live. Success in life must be measured in a more comprehensive manner. For business leaders to be happy, they must learn to balance three significant elements in their lives—spiritual growth, business, and their family values. These must be woven together and threaded through the eye of the needle.

For years I was just as empty and obsessed with money as the men who met in Chicago in 1923. That emptiness eventually brought me to Christ, but it also drove me to identify some crucial principles that govern my attitude toward money. The degree to which I successfully practice these principles is the degree to which I experience the grace of God in my life and business.

Principle One: What's mine isn't mine

Sometime back I learned that everything I have is on loan from God. Like money from the bank, it's mine to use, but it doesn't belong to me.

The ancient Hebrew king said as much when he wrote, "The earth is the Lord's and everything in it, the world, and all who live in it" (Psalm 24:1) Unfortunately, for many years my thinking was like that of the young bride who announced to her husband on their honeymoon, "What's yours is mine, and what's mine is mine too."

A scene in the movie *Wall Street* opens with a tall and handsome man walking to the microphone at a meeting of shareholders. Everything about him declared wealth and power. His suit, his tie, his hairstyle all told the eager crowd that this was a man of importance. And what did he say? He looked at the audience and declared, "Greed is good!"

While few people would openly admit he's right, we've all encountered people who lived as though greed were good.

During the eighties, I rescued a businessman from financial ruin by purchasing his television station. That business deal was the beginning of a friendship that developed over the next few years. When I ran across a strategic opportunity to make us both money, I gave him a call.

"Here's the deal," I said. "I want you to buy a TV station and we'll program it. There is no risk to you. My company will put up all the money and watch over it. Furthermore, my company will buy all the time on the station. You'll have all the money you'll need to operate the station, pay its debt, and pay yourself $100,000 a year."

Obviously, he recognized a great deal when he saw it. And this was a great deal! Later I knew I would sell the station and take the profit. The only thing I asked from him was to accept a $500,000 payment at the time I sold the station.

He agreed—who wouldn't?—and we actually bought two stations in that way. We had a great thing going. At least we did until he allowed greed to destroy our friendship. When it came time to sell the stations, instead of accepting the agreed-upon $500,000 per station, he demanded $2.5 million. In fact, he refused to sign the contract to sell unless I paid him the $2.5 million.

We settled for a little less, but greed ruled the day. He walked away with a lot more money in his pocket, but he compromised his integrity and our friendship.

While greed might not lead us to betray a partner, it still has the power to undermine our integrity. How do we overcome such an insidious force in our lives? One thing we can do is remember that all things belong to God. We are simply managing the assets he places in our keeping. Once we realize that, we can harness greed by putting things in a proper light.

Claude Foster, the founder of the Gabriel Company, understood this principle. He invented the Gabriel Horn for automobiles and founded the company to manufacture it. Years later, he sold the company to a big investment firm for four million dollars, and then did something extraordinary. In celebration, he hosted a party at his house and invited a number of friends who were involved in various charitable causes. The surprise came when he announced, "I am going to give you the $4 million God entrusted to me. Over the years I have come to realize that nothing we earn, none of the things we accumulate, belongs to us. While on earth we are merely stewards or trustees for God's resources. Our job is to handle these resources as wisely as possible and to use what money we have for the good of the greatest number."

Claude Foster understood the principle of stewardship. God had given him the ability to make money just as an employer creates a profit-making environment. Every employee knows the profit he makes is for the company. Regardless of whether he generates $10,000 a year or a million, it all belongs to the company.

As the head of the company, God values us equally, but he has not entrusted us with equal talents and abilities. Some have an abundance of intelligence. Others have musical skills, or artistic skills, or excel in athletics. Some have been given the ability to make money and others the ability to make things. I confess, I don't understand why he gives greater portions to some and less to others. The world is made up of individuals who are uniquely created by God. Regardless of the abilities we possess, it's important to recognize that all things come from God and that He expects us to use them wisely.

His command to Adam and Eve, shortly after creation, was all-encompassing. God told them to manage the earth.

He never intended for them, or us, to lay personal claim to it.

When we begin with the principle that everything belongs to God, it frees us from a bondage to our possessions and helps us to see how we can get the business thread through the needle's eye. It was Francis Bacon who once said of a greedy man, "He does not possess wealth, but wealth possesses him."

Principle Two: Happiness Comes from Giving.

Once we agree that all we have belongs to God, it's easier to release what we have so it can be used for others. The following story illustrates what I mean.

Years ago, a young man started his own business—a dime store at the corner of two streets. Because he was honest and friendly his business grew. In just a short time, he developed his one store into a chain of stores across the country.

Years passed and the man became terminally ill. He called his three adult children together and gave them this challenge: "One of you will become the president of the company. To decide which of you it will be, I am going to give you each a one-dollar bill. Go today and buy whatever you can with that one dollar, but when you get back this evening, whatever you buy with your dollar must fill this room from corner to corner."

The children were excited at the opportunity to run their father's business. Each went to town to spend the dollar. When they came back that evening, the father called the first child in and asked, "What have you done with your dollar?"

"Well, Dad, I went to my friend's farm and bought two bales of hay." With that the son went outside, brought in the hay, loosened the binding, and began throwing the hay all over the room. In a few moments the hay had settled, but the room was not completely filled from corner to corner.

The second child entered and the father asked, "What have you done with your dollar?"

"I went to the store and bought two pillows made with feathers." He tore open the pillows and began spreading the feathers around the room. Soon the feathers had settled but the room was not filled from corner to corner.

The father asked his third child, "And what have you done with your dollar?"

"I took my dollar and went to a store like the one you had years ago," the third child said. "I asked the owner to give me two quarters and five dimes. I gave fifty cents to the soup kitchen, twenty cents to the homeless, and twenty cents to our church. With the dime that was left, I bought two items."

The son then reached into his pocket and took out a candle and a book of matches. He turned off the light switch, lit the candle, and the room was filled with light–from corner to corner.

His father was delighted. "Well done, my son. You will become president of the company because you understand a very important lesson about life. You understand how to let your light shine. That is good." (Nido Quibein, *Chicken Soup for the Soul at Work*, p. 300.)

The challenge the father gave to his children was not about lighting candles. True success comes to those who learn to give away what is not theirs to keep.

In his book *Living Above the Level of Mediocrity*, Chuck Swindoll says, "There is nothing in the world wrong with making a nice living. Nor is there anything wrong with being eminently wealthy if you learn to handle it correctly. But there's something drastically wrong when you keep it all to yourself! God gave it to you so you could, in turn, give it back to Him, to others–yes, in *abundance*. The only reason I can imagine for God's allowing anyone to make more than one needs is to be able to *give* more. We certainly can't take it with us, that's for sure" (p. 158).

I like to relate the story of a rich old man who was dying and told his wife to take all his money, put it in a sack, and hang it in the attic. "When I die and leave this body, I am going to swoop by and grab it on my way, and I'm going to take it with me," he said. Not long after, he died, and she immediately raced to the attic to see if he'd gotten it. Sure enough, the bag was still there. "That old idiot," she said, "I knew I should have put it in the basement."

You can't take it with you. But Jesus says we can send it on ahead. The writer Douglas Lawson wrote, "We exist temporarily through what we take, but we live forever through what we give."

Billy Graham once said, "God has given us two hands: one with which to receive and one with which to give. We are not made for hoarding; we are channels made for sharing." I believe there is something in the way we are made that creates a need to give. Much of our happiness is determined by whether or not we learn how to give.

USE YOUR WEALTH FOR GOD

Once we understand the importance of giving, we must then begin to search out worthy causes. I've traveled around the country speaking to various groups of Christian businessmen with a single challenge: Use your business resources for God, and he will bless your business.

Many hesitate to give a portion of what they have because they feel their contribution is so small. I like the phrase "Little is much when God is in it." If God can turn water to wine and feed five thousand with a small boy's lunch, there is no limit to what he can do when we allocate a portion of our business to serve His kingdom.

Paderewski, the renowned composer-pianist, was scheduled to perform in a majestic concert hall in the United States. It was an evening to remember—a black-tie affair. Present in the audience was a mother with her fidgety nine-year-old son. She was in hopes that her son would be encouraged to practice if he just heard the immortal Paderewski at the keyboard. He, of course, did not share her enthusiasm.

As the audience waited for the performance to begin, the lady turned to talk to friends. Her son could stay in his seat no longer. He slipped away and was strangely drawn to the stage with its ebony Steinway and its leather-tufted stool. Without much notice from anyone, the boy made his way to the stage and sat down on the stool. He placed his small fingers on the keyboard and began to play "Chopsticks." The roar of the crowd was hushed as hundreds of frowning faces pointed in his direction. Irritated and embarrassed, they began to shout:

"Get that boy away from there!"

"Whose child is that?"

"Where's his mother?"

"Someone get him down from there!"

Backstage, the master overheard the sounds out front and quickly put together in his mind what was happening. Hurriedly, he grabbed his coat and rushed toward the stage. Without one word of announcement he stooped over behind the boy, reached around both sides, and began to improvise a countermelody to harmonize and enhance "Chopsticks."

As the two of them played together, Paderewski kept whispering in the boy's ear: "Keep going, don't stop. Keep on playing . . . don't quit . . . don't stop."

And so it is with us. We hammer away in our businesses and give God a portion. At times our gift may seem as insignificant as "Chopsticks" in a concert hall. However, we must remember that little is much when God is involved. He can take our gifts and turn them into something beautiful. For that to happen, we must give him our business resources.

USE WHAT YOU HAVE

Agnes Bojaxhui was raised in Yugoslavia and had very little to offer in the way of resources. When she was twelve years old, Agnes decided she wanted to be a nun. She left home at eighteen and studied in Darjeeling, India, where she joined the Loretto Sisters. For the next twenty years she taught at St. Mary's High School, which was attended primarily by middle-class children.

It was on a train, in 1946, that she felt the call of God to serve the poor in the slums of India. "Soon after leaving Loretto, I was on the street with no shelter, no company, no helper, no money, no employment, no promise, no guarantee, no security," she said. "Then I prayed, 'My God, You, only You. I trust in Your call, Your inspiration. You will not let me down.'"

Her ministry began when she picked up a dying woman from the street and helped her to the hospital. She had been lying in the gutter, and her body had been partly eaten by rats. Mother Teresa then talked the city into giving her space in a former Hindu temple, and she turned it into a home for the dying.

Since then, tens of thousands have been rescued off the streets. In 1979, she won the Nobel Peace Prize, and her name, Mother Teresa, has been synonymous with servanthood. No one would have guessed that the little girl in Yugoslavia would be able to affect the lives of so many. And no one would have imagined that the whole world would mourn her death. Mother Teresa's life stands as a shining example of how God blesses our efforts when we allocate our resources to Him.

When it comes to helping people, everyone has unique talents, abilities, and passions. There is no "one-size-fits-all" in the kingdom of God. And not all ministry has to take place inside the walls of a church. Last year, because our daughter has lupus, my wife, Marla, used her administrative abilities and passion for the Lupus Foundation to organize a fundraiser. Her efforts raised $600,000 for lupus and triggered a national awareness campaign.

Not every opportunity for God is a valid one. Several months ago, while channel surfing, I turned to a well-known televangelist who was raising funds. He demonstrated rare confidence when he told his viewers, "This is the very satellite that will show the scenes to the world when Jesus returns to earth. And your gift can help make the satellite possible."

I was stunned by the absurdity of the claim he made to squeeze money out of his TV audience. What they didn't know (and wouldn't learn from him) was that satellites have limited life expectancy. Unless Christ returns within ten to twelve years, that particular satellite won't carry the event.

Because there are unethical ministries and charities out there, it's crucial we evaluate a charity, church, or ministry before we give it our resources. Because we want to share the message of God's love with everyone, our money needs to be strategically placed.

THE GREAT COMMISSION REQUIRES A GREAT COMMERCE

Mother Teresa once said, "If we really love God, we cannot fail but be consumed with the desire of saving souls, the greatest and dearest interest of Jesus."

The final words of Jesus before he ascended back to heaven were "Go, and make disciples of all nations." Theologians have labeled his words the *Great Commission*. To share the love of God with everyone on earth is going to be an expensive endeavor. I'm convinced the Great Commission is going to require great commerce. Not only do Christians need to tithe their individual incomes, Christian businessmen and women need to tithe their businesses. After all, "The earth is the Lord's and everything in it, the world, and all who live in it." That not only includes what we would consider our personal possessions, but our businesses as well.

I have to constantly remind myself that all I have, and all my company has, belongs to God. We must consciously choose to give a portion of what we have to expand His kingdom. That isn't always easy, but when we do it, we have made great progress in getting our business and spiritual threads through the eye of God's needle.

There has been a lot of discussion in Christian circles about how much we should give. The Bible tells us that from ancient days God required us to give at least a tithe, or ten percent, of our income to his work. It is my opinion that that is a starting place. You are probably thinking, "How can anyone give ten percent of his income or business assets and still survive?" When God developed his program of giving he built into it an exercise of faith. He promises to take care of our needs if we will be obedient in the amount we give.

Obviously, giving a tithe is a tough challenge. That is where God's grace comes in. Remember, it is impossible to get a camel through the eye of a needle, but by God's grace it can be done. You might be amazed at what you can do when you combine obedience and faith with the grace of God.

As I said earlier, God is a God of logic. He expects us to be wise in the way we use his resources and in our eternal investments. I would challenge you to see how you might reinvest your commerce to capitalize the kingdom. It is an investment that pays huge dividends.

Principle Three: Anticipate God's Blessing.

The polished TV evangelist pushed back a lock of his silver hair, turned to the camera with a pleading look, and said, "Child of God, if you will trust in the Lord and send a gift of $25 as seed faith, God will multiply your gift many times over." Not completely sure his message was falling on receptive ears, he managed to create a tear in his eye and repeated his plea. How many times have you heard a message like that? Such distortions give Christianity a bad name and cause the public to be suspicious of anyone who talks about money "in the name of God."

The Bible does make some exciting promises when it comes to giving. It says, "Bring the whole tithe into the storehouse . . . and see if I will not throw open the floodgates of heaven and pour out so much blessing that you will not have room enough for it" (Malachi 3:10). Jesus said, "Give, and it will be given to you. A good measure, pressed down, shaken together and running over, will be poured into your lap. For with the measure you use, it will be measured to you" (Luke 6:38). The Bible is filled with the message that you can't out-give God.

I have been amazed at the reliability of these promises. It's true that God granted me financial success even before I became a Christian, but the fact is He blesses us all. God causes the sun to rise on people who serve him *and* those who don't. He sends rain on those who believe in Him and those who don't. Financial success is not a sign of God's favor, but it is God who gives us the ability to make wealth. After I became a Christian, I recognized that all I have comes from Him. It was a remarkable discovery. When I began to tithe my business, I saw phenomenal growth take place.

On a financial level, Paxson Communications grew beyond my wildest imagination (and continues to grow), but there have been many other blessings, too. It's hard to explain, but my life became richer in many aspects: relationships, my ability to love, a deeper faith, and a sense of personal satisfaction as I helped God meet the needs of others. Unlike some of the messages we hear on TV, God does not promise that all of our blessings will be financial.

When we give with the motive of getting something in return, we negate the promise. God wants us to give from a heart that acknowledges his greatness, expresses our gratitude, and assists in His kingdom endeavors. He is not a cosmic genie who doles out blessings because we rubbed the magic lamp with our financial gifts. He knows our heart and our motive. People are not likely to see the blessings of God when they give with selfish intentions.

As a Christian businessman I would challenge you to take inventory of your possessions. The rich young man came to Jesus wanting to know what he must do to inherit eternal life. He wanted to get his camel through the needle. Jesus explained that only by God's grace can we get to heaven, but he recognized a fatal flaw in the young man's character. He thought his possessions were his own and he didn't want to give them away.

I close this chapter by clearly stating a business principle I believe in and try to live by. First, I must give a word of caution. It will only work in a business where the leadership has a commitment to the Lordship of Christ.

Here is the principle: If you'll ask God to lead you in serving Him with your business, job, or career, you'll be successful beyond your wildest dreams. Just writing a business or personal check to a worthy charitable cause won't work. But if you devote capital, profits, resources, plus management's skills and time to God's cause . . . look out! Your company, job, or career will be enriched. Why? Because God will help you so you can devote more capital, profit, time resources, and management to His cause. There is no limit, as far as I can see. Our company is living proof. PAX NET is proof.

11

INTEGRITY . . .
VALUE-DRIVEN DECISIONS

In order to launch PAX NET we felt we needed to find a program that would attract younger viewers. A number of people on my staff suggested we consider buying the syndication rights to *Party of Five*. Negotiations were started, but before making a decision I needed to watch a sampling of episodes. Columbia Tri-Star was nice enough to send me not only several episodes, but a *Party of Five* jacket, hat, and golf shirt. I could have looked like a walking commercial, but I gave the gifts to my daughter, Nicole. When I mentioned that we might air the show, she was ecstatic.

"Oh, Dad, that's wonderful," she said. "That's the coolest show in America."

"Tell me about it," I said.

"Well, Dad, I love the cast. And the stories are fun to watch. But . . . "

"But what?" I asked.

"Well, I thought you were going to avoid sex and violence."

While my daughter liked the show, she realized it was inconsistent with the family values of PAX NET. After we viewed a handful of shows, I agreed. Unfortunately, before we had viewed the tapes, the press got wind that we were considering the program, and a lot of criticism followed. Once that happened I felt we needed to clear the air. To accomplish that

I decided to announce the acquisition of a big show that fell in line with our values. Since that announcement was being made anyway, I decided to hide a single line in it noting that we wouldn't continue to negotiate with *Party of Five*.

The next day I discovered a network had never in the history of television issued a press release saying they were no longer negotiating for a show. Normally, if a deal isn't reached, the story just disappears.

Shortly after the press announcement appeared, Columbia Tri-Star called. "How could you publish that story?" they asked.

"We didn't leak the information about the negotiations," I said. "You did." I then told them I put the press release out to get the critics off my back and to correct the campaign of disinformation that had started. The rumors about our acquiring *Party of Five* indicated we had abandoned our commitment to family values. I wanted the public to know that we had not. Well, I got a real tongue-lashing and was informed PAX NET would never be allowed to do business with Columbia Tri-Star. Six months later we patched up the relationship and entered negotiations for PAX NET daytime programming.

UNDERSTANDING PRINCIPLES AND VALUES

The decision not to purchase *Party of Five* was fairly easy once we understood the nature of the show. Through the lengthy process of building PAX NET and making such choices, I wrestled with the issue of integrity in a fresh way. Time and again I reminded myself that I was trying to thread the needle. I knew doing so would require clinging to the values that please God.

In the last chapter I noted the importance of making sure

a decision is in keeping with the moral laws, or principles of God, as revealed in the Bible. These principles are more than rules or codes of conduct. A principle is a comprehensive and governing law of life. It's timeless in that it's always been true. And it's universal in that it's true everywhere—from Europe to Asia, to Africa, to the Americas. Take honesty, for instance. It's not something that is morally right to practice in Miami but not in Washington, D.C. It's always right to be honest no matter where a person might be.

Having said that, it's important to realize principles and values are not the same thing. A principle is something outside of a person. It's true whether or not someone believes it. The law of gravity is a principle that says objects have weight and that's why they fall when dropped. The reliability of the law of gravity does not depend on whether or not someone believes in it. The principles of God's moral laws are the same, except they address a spiritual rather than a natural reality. The ten commandments apply to everyone—regardless of whether or not they're accepted as reliable.

While principles are outside of us, values are within us. A value is an internalized principle. A person may acknowledge that God's moral principles are true, without internalizing them. Such a person would say, "I believe lying is wrong." Yet they consistently lie. That individual hasn't transformed God's principle into a value.

THE SURPRISE QUESTION

A friend recently told me a story about two sophomores at Duke University. Throughout the fall semester they made A's on all of the quizzes and papers in an Organic Chemistry class.

They were so confident going into the final exam that the weekend before finals they decided to go to the University of

Virginia to party with some friends. They had a blast Saturday night but ended up drinking so much that they slept in on Sunday and didn't get back to Duke until early Monday morning. Rather than taking the final, they found the professor and lied about what happened.

"We went to UV for the weekend and planned on getting back for the exam," one of them said. "But a tire blew out and we didn't have a spare. We had to wait by the car for an hour before someone finally stopped to help us. By the time we got another tire there was no way we could get here for the test without driving way too fast."

Smiling, the professor asked, "You're telling the truth?"

"Of course we are."

"All right. You can come by my office on Wednesday at 3:00 P.M. and take a makeup exam."

The two walked away elated and relieved. Throughout the rest of Monday and all of Tuesday they studied for the final. At precisely 3:00 P.M. on Wednesday they showed up for the exam. The professor ushered them into separate rooms and handed them each a test.

They both easily answered the first question, which was worth five points. At almost the same time they both smiled and said, "Cool! This is going to be easy."

Upon turning to the second page they discovered the only other question on the test—it was worth ninety-five points. It asked, "Which tire was flat?"

In a short time their professor would discover that honesty was a principle for those students, not a value. They both knew it was important, but they hadn't internalized it. Soon they would discover the high price of violating the principle of honesty.

I believe God's moral laws are reliable. But I desire to go the next step. I want to internalize the principles of his moral

laws so they govern the way I run a business. I want my decisions to be based on what's right, rather than what's easy.

Before we decided that PAX NET would go it alone, we
considered joining forces with other networks and programming entities. We talked with the leaders at NBC, ABC, Fox,
and Turner. After each meeting, Dean Goodman, the president of PAX NET, and I would walk away impressed with
their creative ideas and potential programming. And then one
of us would ask the other, "How can we maintain family values and run their programs?" And then a second question was
asked: "When we tell them we intend to keep *Worship* on
overnight, what will they say?"

We knew that there was no way we could partner with any
of them—even though it would have been the easiest course
of action. Joining ranks with one of them would have forced
us to abandon our belief that television should be used to
build up the family, not tear it down.

"What about profit?" you might ask. The only advantage
a partner would have given us was a quick solution to our programming problem. Turning down the networks didn't put
PAX NET at risk or keep it from profits. We own over a billion dollars in television stations that we bought rather inex-
pensively. The struggle I faced didn't concern the profitability
of the network. It was a choice between making the right decision and making the easy one with PAX NET.

I'm convinced if we make morally correct decisions that
also reflect good business sense, we'll make a profit. In fact, I
believe we'll make a substantial profit.

THE MEANING OF INTEGRITY

Such decisions aren't always easy, but maintaining integrity is
vital. The words "integrity" and "integrated" come from the

same root word. When something is "integrated" it's blended together into a unified whole. An integrated school is one in which students of different races come together to form a student body. The word "integrity" speaks of persons who have integrated their inner and outer selves. They are on the inside what they appear to be on the outside.

There is a story about a man who was dying. One day he called in his three best friends and said, "You're the best buddies I have in the entire world. I've decided to give each of you $1 million. You can invest it any way you want. But when I die, I want it placed in my casket and buried with me."

Nine months later, at the man's funeral, each of his buddies placed a briefcase in the casket. After the funeral the three met at a local restaurant to share stories about their departed friend. Eventually, the conversation got around to the money.

"I need to tell you guys that I only put $600,000 in the briefcase," one of them confessed.

"I only put in $500,000," the second said.

Shaking his head in disbelief, the third one said, "You two guys disgust me. How could you do something like that? He was our best friend. I want you to know I was absolutely true to my word. I placed a check for the entire $1 million in the briefcase."

While the third friend may have sounded more honest, he wasn't on the inside what he appeared to be on the outside. He lacked integrity.

COMPASSES AND WEATHER VANES

A person with integrity is more like a compass than a weather vane. Both instruments are made of a needle on a swivel. The difference is that the internal makeup of a compass is such that it always points due north, while a weather vane changes direction with the wind.

A lot of political and business leaders remind me of weather vanes. Before making a decision they determine the wind direction of popular opinion. They then base their decisions on what others want, rather than on what is right. Because their lives aren't guided by moral principles that they've internalized, shifting political winds control their decisions.

Like a compass, people of integrity don't allow circumstances to dictate their behavior. An internal compass governs their behavior—one that's controlled by moral values.

History's greatest leaders were all compasses. People looked to them for moral direction. Winston Churchill refused to allow the evil of the Nazi regime to overwhelm Great Britain. Mother Teresa refused to waver from her commitment to provide love to the dying of India. Martin Luther King, Jr., did not let the unpopularity of his views on integration slow him down.

LINCOLN . . . A MORAL COMPASS

For the last twenty years, when asked to list the greatest leaders in the history of the United States, Americans have placed Abraham Lincoln's name at the top of the list. When it came to matters of slavery, he stood his ground. Regardless of what others said, he refused to compromise right. People trusted Lincoln because they always knew where he stood. And the strength of his character enabled him to lead our nation through one of its most difficult struggles.

It would be easy to think great leaders, like Abraham Lincoln, are born leaders. Such isn't the case. Character is something that's developed over the course of a lifetime. At PAX NET we want our commitment to family values to be seen in our programming. Hopefully, by providing such programming, our own character, the character of television, and that of our nation will be strengthened.

WHAT DOES TV TELL OUR KIDS?

Of course, I recognize that integrity isn't something that is developed simply by watching television. However, television can undermine or strengthen our moral values. And frankly, most parents are not concerned about the amount of sexual content and violence on television, especially during prime time. Recent research indicates they should be concerned. Instead of turning children away, the new TV rating system may actually attract youngster to violent or sexually explicit shows. In a report released in March 1998, researchers from four universities also concluded that cartoons and other children's TV programs rarely show the real consequences of violence.

VIOLENCE WITHOUT CONSEQUENCES

Unfortunately, things are not getting better. The level of violence during the 1995–1996 television season was higher than the previous year. Researchers identified over 18,000 violent incidents in a sample of more than 2,000 hours drawn from 23 cable and broadcast channels.

In 40 percent of all violent incidents, the violence is glamorized and is committed by characters who are attractive role models. Seventy-one percent of violent scenes contain no remorse, criticism, or penalty for violence, and "bad" characters go unpunished in 37 percent of programs. Equally harmful is the fact that in more than half of all violent incidents the victim is not shown suffering any pain. (From an article dated March 26, 1997, that was posted on CNN Interactive, *Showbiz Story Page.* The conclusions are based on research at the University of

California at Santa Barbara, the University of North Carolina, the University of Texas, and the University of Wisconsin.)

SEX WITHOUT RESPONSIBILITY

More children watch TV during prime time than on Saturday mornings or weekday afternoons. In fact, seventeen of the top twenty-five programs watched by children two to eleven are aired during prime time. Based on a report commissioned by the Kaiser Family Foundation and Children Now, in 1996 sixty-one percent of family-hour shows contain sexual behavior, up from 48 percent in 1986 and 26 percent in 1976.

All of this sexual activity occurs in a setting where only 9 percent of sexual scenes had any mention of issues relating to morality, sexual risks, or responsibilities. None of the examples of sex in the study were linked with any discussion of a man or woman's responsibility. (The statistical data presented or gleaned from an article reprinted on the *Media Awareness Network,* which was commissioned by Children Now and the Kaiser Family Foundation. Full copies of the report can be obtained from either organization.)

On a typical night 13.1 million children seventeen and younger are watching prime-time shows. I'm convinced this repeated exposure to acts of violence and sex leads to a desensitization of our children. How could they not be affected in this way? By early adolescence children have viewed more than 8,000 killings and 100,000 other violent acts on television.

In a study released in June 1997 to the Ohio Department of Mental Health, Professors Mark J. Singer and David B. Miller of Case Western Reserve University reported that children in grades three though eight who watch significantly more television than their peers display the highest propensity toward psychological trauma. Violence on TV may or may not cause children to act more violently, but it certainly can become a destructive way for kids to escape. (Based on a July 14, 1997, article by Columbus *Dispatch* television critic Julia Keller, entitled "Monkey See, Monkey Do Debate Targets Sex, Violence," which was found on the Internet.)

Why have I mentioned these negative facts about sex and violence on television? Because our children are spending hours learning from the examples they see on television. As parents we should be asking whether or not these prime-time role models are providing our kids with examples of honesty and integrity. We should question if they're demonstrating an internal moral compass that enables them to do right even when tempted to do wrong. Occasionally, a television star provides an excellent example of honesty and integrity. But all too often they live like weather vanes on TV, making decisions based on peer pressure or pleasure.

At PAX NET we want to provide both parents and children with heroes who provide positive role models. Ultimately, integrity is developed from the inside out and reinforced by what we choose to watch on television. But the choices we make every day, including what we watch on TV, tell us what we truly value.

If someone says they believe honesty and morality are important principles of life, they need to run an internal scan to see if they have made those principles values. How do they do that? By examining how they make choices.

HONESTY OR FAMILY?

For instance, a friend of mine who lives on the West Coast has a son attending college in Chicago. One day a buddy of his offered to fly the two of them to the Windy City so they could watch his son play soccer. Needless to say, my friend looked forward to a great weekend.

Several weeks later he realized that he had committed himself to be the keynote speaker at a banquet on the same day they were scheduled to visit Chicago. Hoping to bow out of the speaking engagement, he called the host of the event.

"Richard, I'm afraid I'm going to have to back out of the banquet. I'll be in Chicago," he said.

"You're kidding. Right?"

"No. I've got a conflict and I can't be there."

The moment my friend hung up the phone he realized what he had done. He had proven that time with his son was more important than honesty. He acknowledged the principle of honesty, but wasn't acting like it was a value.

Less than a minute later, he picked up the phone again and called the host of the banquet, "Richard, forget everything I said before. I'll be there."

Why had my friend made the second call? Because he knew that it was more important to be honest than to spend time with his son. Just as we knew it was more important to go it alone as a network than acquire easy programming with a partner. Especially if that programming meant PAX NET would have to abandon family values by showing sex and violence.

Every day we all make decisions that reveal what we truly value. If we value honesty and morality, then we'll search for shows on TV that reinforce those values. If we value the thrill of vicarious violence and sexual pleasure, then we'll turn to shows that give us those. Our choices are a foolproof test of our values.

"YOU'LL DO!"

Because we never know when our integrity will be tested, it's a good idea to consistently check our internal compass and make sure we're headed in the right direction. That's a lesson learned by a rookie nurse one day. In the operating room of a large hospital, she was completing her first full day of responsibilities. As the surgeon snapped off his surgical gloves he told her to close the incision.

"But doctor, you've only removed eleven sponges. We used twelve."

"I removed them all," the doctor declared. "Now close the incision."

"No!" the nurse objected. "We used twelve sponges and there are only eleven on the table."

"I'll take full responsibility," the surgeon said sternly. "Suture!"

"You can't do that!" blazed the nurse. "Think of the patient."

The surgeon smiled, lifted his foot, and showed the nurse the twelfth sponge, which he had hidden under his shoe. Smiling, he said, "You'll do."

That nurse didn't expect a parade or her name in lights for her unwillingness to compromise right. She was just doing her duty. After all, it's expected of doctors and nurses to remove sponges from patients.

But a person of integrity, someone who has made honesty and morality a value, will be willing to risk her job or reputation to make sure every sponge is accounted for. That's the kind of integrity that should drive all of our decisions. And it's the kind of integrity that needs to be translated into the practices of a business.

AN OPPORTUNITY FOR INTEGRITY

A lot of naysayers and critics contend that starting another network is like picking a fight that can't be won. They believe there isn't a market for the family-oriented programming of

PAX NET. Frankly, when I look at the deluge of trashy programming that's flooding the market today, I don't believe for a second we can fail. Many people look at the tide of violence and sex in television and feel they have to swim with that tide. I look at it and say the volume of antifamily programming is so great it's created a huge need for what we offer.

I'm reminded of the story of the twin boys who were identical in every way except their temperament. One was an optimist and the other was a pessimist. On their sixth birthday their parents decided to give the boys a pony. But instead of simply handing the animal over to them, the parents decided to do something more creative.

Without telling the boys, they had a truckload of horse manure dumped in the barn. On the big day the two boys were led out to the barn that was situated behind their country home. The pessimistic son was then led into the barn and left there alone. A few minutes later he walked out, shaking his head in disgust and saying, "That's the meanest thing anybody has ever done to me."

The optimist was then led into the barn and the door was closed. Five minutes passed without a word from him. Ten minutes passed without a sign from the boy. After twenty minutes the father opened the barn door and saw his son vigorously shoveling horse manure.

As the manure flew in the air the boy shouted back at his dad, "With this much horse manure, there must be a pony somewhere!"

I'm convinced that hidden beneath the pile of moral manure on television today is an opportunity—an opportunity to provide Americans with values-driven programming. Such programming will create role models and encourage them to look to God to help them use their own moral compass. And as they do that, they'll discover others will benefit greatly.

12

SERVICE . . .
HELPING OTHERS

Andrew Carnegie said, "No man can become rich without himself enriching others." Carnegie lived that philosophy, as evidenced by the 43 millionaires he had working for him. One day a reporter asked Mr. Carnegie how he was able to hire so many rich men.

"I didn't hire them," he said. "They became millionaires working for me."

Curious, the reporter asked a follow-up question. "How were you able to develop those men to the point where they created so much wealth?"

"When you work with people it's a lot like mining for gold," Carnegie answered. "Miners will move tons of dirt to find a single ounce of gold. However, they aren't looking for dirt. They're looking for gold."

I'm convinced that threading the needle involves serving others in a way that enables them to tap their God-given and often hidden potential. Service is a fundamental principle of leadership that needs to become a value.

Jesus himself said he had not come to be served but to serve. On a couple of occasions he corrected his disciples because they held to the idea that a leader is to lord it over other people. Not everyone is called by God and directed by the Holy Spirit to be an entrepreneur. "Do not think of yourself more highly than you ought, but rather think of yourself with sober judgment, in accordance with the measure of faith

God has given you. . . We have different gifts, according to the grace given us" (Romans 12:3 & 6).

At PAX NET we don't want to just give lip service to the service concept. We want to put it into practice. Our ambition is to serve our customers—the American public—and our employees. I'm convinced we do that when we practice several principles.

First: We serve others best when we serve God first.

The psalmist underlined the importance of maintaining the proper focus when he said, "*Unless the Lord builds the house, its builders labor in vain*" (Psalm 127:1). It's crucial that the focus of an enterprise not be the organizing and managing of a project or team. It can't be the profit that will be generated, although that is important. The focus throughout the beginning, middle and end of an enterprise must be to serve God.

All sorts of things will clamor for our attention and beg for our devotion. During the time of the American Revolution one particular man seemed destined for greatness. When he was fourteen years old he ran away from home to fight in the French and Indian War. Later, he became a captain in the Connecticut militia. At the outbreak of the Revolutionary War he rallied volunteers and joined the freedom-fighting settlers as a colonel in the army.

Bravery and heroics marked his career. He shared a command with Ethan Allen in the capture of Ticonderoga. In 1775 he led 1,000 men into Canada to fight the British. His leg was broken in the battle against Quebec and his courage won him a promotion to brigadier general. In the Second Battle of Saratoga he was badly wounded. This time the Congress voted him the country's thanks and promoted him to major general. In harmony with his great military career he married a high-society girl from Philadelphia.

Without a doubt, this man was destined to become a national superstar. But something went wrong. Thoughts of compromise began to eat away at his patriotic zeal. His devotion to the new republic was replaced with a desire for money—the British offered him a large payment for his services.

In 1780 his plot to hand over West Point to the British army was uncovered. Later, he actually led the British army in the burning of Richmond, Virginia, and New London, Connecticut. Rather than being recognized as a great American hero, Benedict Arnold is remembered as the most infamous traitor in American history. His name has become a synonym for the word "traitor." Sadly, he died discouraged, distrusted and in debt.

That's the tragedy of compromise. It robs us of the best. It destroys our hopes for the future. It erases our dreams. Because none of us is immune to compromise, it's crucial we keep our focus on God. Otherwise, we will find ourselves given to less important passions. Ultimately, we serve others best when we serve God first. Anyone can start and run a business and even generate a measure of profit. However, I believe it's crucial that we be called by God into a particular business and continually seek to please him in the way we run it. I like the words of Paul, who said, "Since we live by the Spirit, let us keep in step with the Spirit" (Galatians 5:25).

As we do that, we'll discover that the opportunities we have are in keeping with our abilities. In other words, God will only call us to do that which we are able to perform. The wonder of being an entrepreneur who is linked with God is that there are virtually no risks. Why? Because once a decision is made, in keeping with the principles articulated in chapter nine, a person can safely assume God is behind his or her endeavor. If that's the case, there will be the assurance that God is accomplishing *His* purpose through the effort. When you are led by the Spirit, you will accomplish things you would not think possible. "A man's steps are directed by the Lord. How then can anyone understand his own way?" (Proverbs 20:24).

Second, we serve others best when we serve without stress.

One day I saw a cartoon that consisted of a single picture. In the middle of the frame was a large blender filled with water and a fish. With a wide-eyed, panicked look, the fish says, "I can't stand it!"

Talk about stress. That poor fish lives with the constant reality that at any minute he could be ripped into a thousand pieces. I suspect that cartoon captures the feelings of a lot of entrepreneurs. They're surrounded by so many pressures that on almost any day, they feel they could be ripped apart by the blades of financial failure. It may be that you feel like that fish as you read these words.

Stress is basically the way our bodies respond to real or perceived danger. Our blood pressure skyrockets and our muscle strength increases. We're ready to stay and fight or turn and run.

If we were in a truly dangerous situation such a response would be appropriate. If someone broke into my house at night I think it would be okay for me to feel some stress. The problem is, we often feel stress when there is no present danger to our safety or lives.

How do we cope with such stress in the marketplace? I can't pretend I don't struggle with stress. But I've discovered that prayer is the safety valve that allows me to release stress in a constructive way. It reminds me that God is in control and will take care of problems that are beyond my reach. No verse in the Bible communicates this idea better than the one that says, "Do not be anxious about anything, but in everything, by prayer and petition, with thanksgiving, present your requests

to God. And the peace of God, which transcends all understanding, will guard your hearts and your minds in Christ
Jesus" (Philippians 4:6–7). God never intended you to take on
the risks of a business venture. He wants you to unload them
on him. I've found that nothing helps me release stress like
talking with God and handing my problems off to him.

*Three: We serve others by making a profit in a way that helps
the American family.*

While profit isn't the primary motivation behind a business, it is the byproduct of a business that pleases God. When
Jesus spoke about the acquisition of the world's goods he said,
"Seek first his kingdom and his righteousness, and all these
things will be given to you as well" (Matthew 6:33). God will
bring the profit as we put him first. "The blessing of the Lord
brings wealth, and he adds no trouble to it" (Proverbs 10:22)

One way to pursue profit is to do it in a manner that
builds others up instead of tearing them down. At PAX NET
we're going to do that by giving the public access to programming that supports family values. "But does the American
public want family programming?" someone may ask. The
ratings of *Touched by an Angel* indicate that they do. I don't
think someone has to be a rocket scientist or psychologist to
figure out we're a product of our upbringing and environment. Certainly if someone sits in front of a television for
hours every day it will affect him or her as a person.

I noted in the last chapter that the amount of sex and violence on television is increasing. Day after day the American
public is exposed to violence against family, friends, teachers
and police. The repeated exposures to these excesses have a tendency to harden us. We begin to think violence is a part of life.

In regards to sex, the idea is communicated time and
again that recreational sex and adultery are acceptable. We see
them as a part of life. They happen. So if they happen, and

everything turns out well, then recreational sex and adultery must be okay. If sexual immorality is viewed as nothing more than an alternative lifestyle, then our kids are led to believe they can act out their sexual tendencies.

I believe there is a message that is more helpful to the public. It's the message that love, marriage and sex go together. Sex channeled into the boundary of marriage is a wonderful thing. But allowed to overflow the banks of marriage, it can consume and destroy an individual and nation.

Because most of the networks believe the American public has an insatiable appetite for sex and violence, they give them an increasing diet of it. Furthermore, they continually try to find something more shocking than what went before. This has led some networks to provide their affiliates with video footage of people actually getting hit by a car, shot by a gang member, falling from a plane and burning alive. No longer are they content to provide simulated violence and sex—they are now offering the real thing.

At PAX NET we don't believe the solution is government censorship. Rather, we believe the solution is to provide the public with an alternative—an alternative we believe the majority of the American public both wants and needs.

Four: We serve others by affirming their efforts.

What does this mean? It means if you value the people around you, catch them doing something good and praise them for it. It's funny how everybody with a dog understands and practices this fundamental rule of behavior. Our family dog is a beautiful 80-pound Rottweiler named Bubba. We house-trained him with the same technique used by millions of other dog owners. Every act of good behavior was immediately followed with words of praise and affirmation. If we waited several hours after a performance to pat his head and say, "Good dog," he'd like the affection, but it would be meaningless.

If you value the people on your team, tell them. Let them know they are your greatest asset. As you do, not only will they thrive, but so will your company and its reputation.

Five: We serve others by pursuing excellence in all we do.

Few stories illustrate the impact excellence can have on those we serve better than the one told by Petey Parker. He had flown to Dallas for the purpose of calling on one client. Time was of the essence and his plan included a quick turnaround trip and then back to the airport. A spotless cab pulled up to the curb. The driver rushed to open the passenger door for him and made sure he was comfortably seated before he closed it. As he got into the driver's seat, he mentioned that the neatly folded *Wall Street Journal* next to Petey was for his use. He then showed him several audiotapes and asked what type of music he preferred.

Petey said he looked around to see if he could spot the hidden camera. He figured he had to be on *Candid Camera*. He couldn't believe the service he was receiving.

"You take great pride in your work," he said to the driver. "You must have a story to tell."

"I used to be in corporate America," he began. "But I got tired of thinking my best would never be good enough, fast enough, or appreciated enough. I decided to find my niche in life where I could feel proud of being the best I could be. I knew I would never be a rocket scientist, but I love driving cars, being of service, and feeling like I have done a full day's work and done it well."

After evaluating his personal assets, he decided to become a cab driver. "Not just a regular taxi hack," he said, "but a professional cab driver. One thing I know for sure, to be good in my business I could simply just meet the expectations of my passengers. But to be great in my business, I'd have to exceed the customer's expectations. I like the sound of being 'great' better than just getting by on 'average.'"

When Petey Parker got out of the cab, he dug deep into his pocket and left that "professional cab driver" a tip that expressed how much he appreciated the excellence in service. (from *Chicken Soup for the Soul at Work,* Jack Canfield, Mark Victor Hansen, Maida Rogerson, Martin Rutte & Tim Clauss, Health Communications, Inc., Deerfield Beach, FL, 1996, pp. 123–124.)

As a television network we know that we must provide excellence in service. But we want to exceed the public's expectations. We want to give them quality in programming *and* service.

A lot of people think I'm trying to create a Christian television network. That is *not* true! PAX NET is not a Christian network. It's a network that will use drama about life to strengthen family values while letting people know that God loves them. It will entertain as well as show values.

Television can't replace the church in people's lives. Spiritual growth occurs when the ingredients of Bible study, fellowship and prayer are present. These are the attributes of a church, not a TV set.

Sometimes I'll hear someone say, "Wow! TV is the great mass communication system." Sure it is. But we aren't trying to create a television church that looks to PAX NET for nurturing. Excellence for us involves giving the American public the best family-oriented programs available. That's why we went after *Touched by an Angel, Dr. Quinn, Medicine Woman, Promised Land, Highway to Heaven, Bonanza, Diagnosis Murder, Seventh Heaven, Life Goes On* and other programs that have proven popular.

Six: We serve others by releasing their creativity and imagination.

Absolutely nothing is more important to the development of a business than the creativity of its people. Remember, every new device and technology began as an idea in someone's mind. In a field like television, imagination rules. Since that's the case, it's crucial for our business to serve the members of our team by encouraging their creativity.

As we do this, our company will flourish. In her autobiography, *Angels Along the Way,* Della Reese tells a story about her conductor and arranger, Peter Meyers, and the effect he had on her life because he turned loose her creativity.

Until he entered her life, Della always felt inhibited in musical ideas because she had no formal musical training. Because she had an excellent ear, an understanding of harmony and years of experience directing gospel choirs, Della had a sense about how a song should sound. In fact, she said she could actually hear the instrumentation in her head that produced the feeling she wanted the song to have. By mentally transposing what she knew from vocal arranging, she might use the soprano part for the trumpet, or the alto part for the strings, or the contralto for the higher saxes and the baritones and bass for the lower saxes.

Whenever she told an arranger what she wanted in the song, he would tell her, "You can't do that," or, "That's not musically correct." Since they were the musical "experts," she just backed off. But the songs remained in her head.

Early in her association with Peter Meyers they were working out a new song and she made an arrangement suggestion. Before he could respond she said, "I guess that's not musically correct."

"What do you mean?"

"Well, uh, you can't do that, huh? I mean, I know I can hear it, but it can't be played, right?"

"If you can hear it, I can play it. Just sing me what you hear."

She did and he played it just the way she had been hearing it. That moment was a musical awakening for Della, who until then had been told her arranging ideas were impossible to perform.

Peter then offered her words of encouragement. "What they should have told you was that they weren't capable of doing it. Because if you can hear it, it is musically correct. It wasn't you, Della."

That experience liberated Della to freely express what she thought a song should sound like. And it made for a stronger musical relationship with Peter Meyers. (*Angels Along the Way,* Della Reese, G.P. Putnam's Sons, New York, NY, 1997, pp. 232–233.)

We serve others best when we turn loose their God-given creativity.

Seven: We serve others by providing them with opportunities to move ahead.

In the early nineties I met a man who owned radio stations in Detroit, Jacksonville, Florida and Kansas City. For several decades this man had experienced tremendous success in the radio business. And then in 1991 the industry nosedived by some 25%. During that time it was next to impossible to borrow money for radio stations because of some restrictive banking rules. Consequently, banks were foreclosing on radio stations as never before.

When I talked with this man I discovered the stations owed the IRS, they owed their lawyers, they owed banks and they even owed him money. Eventually, everybody got paid off but this guy. He received absolutely nothing. Nada!

Because I had been through a few tough times myself I knew how he was feeling. We spent considerable time together and I discovered he understood the radio business better than anybody I knew. His problem was that he had been dealt a poor hand by the business climate. Realizing his potential, I hired him to run our radio group and he did such a great job that he now is president of Paxson Television Stations Group.

Men like Jay Hoker are one of the key reasons our company has been able to grow at such an astounding rate. One of our jobs is to find talented people and then serve them by placing them in positions where they can succeed. One way we do that is by appreciating what they contribute.

Several years ago *Newsweek* ran an immensely valuable two-page piece entitled, "Advice to a (Bored) Young Man" in its "Responsibility Series." Despite its title, the counsel of the story is appropriate for every business. In fact, it's appropriate for all of us.

Died, age 20; buried, age 60. The sad epitaph of too many Americans. Mummification sets in on too many young men at an age when they should be ripping the world wide open. For example: Many people reading this page are doing so with the aid of bifocals, Inventor *B. Franklin*, age 79.

The presses that printed this page were powered by electricity. One of the first harnessers? *B. Franklin*, age 40.

Some are reading this on the campus of one of the Ivy League universities. Founder? *B. Franklin*, age 25.

Some got their copy through the U.S. Mail. Its father? *B. Franklin*, age 31.

Now, think fire. Who started the first fire department, invented the lightning rod, designed a heating stove still in use today? *B. Franklin*, ages 31, 43, 36.

Wit, Conversationalist, Economist, Philosopher, Diplomat, Printer, Publisher, Linguist (spoke and wrote five languages). Advocate of paratroopers (from balloons) a century before the airplane was invented. All this until age 84.

And he had exactly two years of formal schooling. It's a good bet that you already have more sheer knowledge than Franklin ever had when he was your age.

Perhaps you think there's no use trying to think of anything new, that everything's been done. Wrong. The simple, agrarian America of Franklin's day didn't begin to need the answers we need today. Go do something about it.

Newsweek then suggested that the readers tear out the page and "read it on your 84th birthday. Ask yourself what took over your life; indolence or ingenuity." ["Advice to a (Bored) Young Man," *Newsweek,* February 13, 1967.]

We believe that we serve our employees best by providing them with a setting in which, like B. Franklin, they can achieve any dream God gives them.

How do I go about putting the PAX NET credo into practice? How do I go about using my resources to help others? It's not always easy, but I think the following story will help explain.

One day a little boy was helping his father stack some wood cut from a fallen tree. The little boy reached down and tried to pick up a piece of wood that was just about as big as he was. He grunted and groaned and then stopped, exhausted. He couldn't move it. Desperate, he called out to his father, "Daddy, I can't move it!"

The man answered, "Well, Son, are you using all your strength?"

The little boy said, "Yes." Not to be outdone by a piece of wood, he braced himself and grabbed it with a fresh sense of determination. He grunted and groaned and managed to lift it a few inches off the ground, only to drop it again. He began to cry and said, "Daddy, I can't lift it."

"Son, are you using all your strength?"

"Yes, Daddy," he said, wiping his eyes.

"No, you're not, Son. You haven't asked me."

"Daddy, will you help me?"

"Sure, Son."

Together, they lifted the log with ease, because the boy used all of the strength available to him.

Often, when I contemplate the challenge of serving others, I feel like that boy. Yet I'm learning that getting the thread of service through the needle can only be accomplished as I tap into the grace and strength of God. "Trust in the Lord with all your heart and lean not on your own understanding; in all your ways acknowledge him, and he will make your paths straight" (Proverbs 3:5–6).

13

ANGELS AND MODERN-DAY MIRACLES

Are angels real? I believe they are. Do miracles happen? I think so.

I'm not one of those guys who believes every unusual event is a miracle. I just don't think that way. Was it a miracle when I prayed about *must carry* and got a sense of knowing from God . . . a knowing that urged me "not to worry about *must carry?*" I don't see that as a miracle.

If someone has been diagnosed with cancer of the lungs and the x-rays revealed a massive and inoperable tumor, the only hope for that person would be prayer. If after prayer that person returned to the doctor and new x-rays showed the tumor had disappeared—I would call that a miracle.

Do miracles occur nowadays? I'm sure they do. However, I must say that I've never personally prayed for someone with a clearly diagnosed disease and had him or her healed by God. But I have no problem believing that could happen.

Most Americans believe in miracles. We believe God is both able and willing to periodically interrupt the natural flow of things with a supernatural act–an act that accomplishes something that couldn't have been accomplished without divine intervention.

And what about angels? A 1996 Gallup Poll revealed that 72 percent of American adults believe in angels, up from 56 percent in 1978.

Why are the people of our country so interested in angels?

One student of American culture suggests that a lot of us, especially American women, have a heightened sense of, "Who's going to take care of me? And who better than someone above this world?" (Carla Johnson, assistant professor of communications at St. Mary's College, as quoted in the *Chicago Tribune,* "A Wing and a Prayer," by Marya Smith, 12/21/97.) I suspect the approach of the new millennium has surfaced a spiritual interest that was dormant a few years ago—an interest that has translated into a curiosity about the beings who occupy the unseen world.

Regardless of what's causing the recent interest in angels, its presence is apparent everywhere. All you have to do is walk down the aisles of a bookstore and you'll see books bearing such names as *An Angel a Day, Angels Over Their Shoulders, Angels . . . Guardians of Light,* and, simply, *Angels.* Television talk shows have caught on to the interest and added to it by hosting guests who claim to have seen angels, communicated with angels, or hand-made angel dolls.

I'm convinced the hit television show *Touched by an Angel,* which will be the program cornerstone of PAX NET, has played a major role in our country's growing interest in angels. And I'm thankful that those who produce the show seek to present angels in a manner that is harmonious with what the Bible says about them. In fact, I think one reason the show has been so popular is that it presents angels as messengers of God rather than the souls of dead people.

Frankly, I believe if I'm going to thread the needle I have to maintain a reliable and balanced view of the spiritual world—including angels. If I ignore God and his messengers, then I run the risk of missing an impression that will help me make a wise decision. Or I may miss his assistance and strength during a time of emotional, psychological, or spiritual need.

A perceptive reader may ask, "Why are you talking about miracles and angels in a section of the book where you're dealing with values?" Or, to put it differently, "In what way are modern-day miracles and angels *values*?" Remember, a principle is a universal and timeless truth—such as "miracles occur and angels are present." A value is an internalized principle. When I personally believe God can do the miraculous and accept the presence of angels, then the principle has become a value. In this chapter I want us to examine two questions about angels that will help us maintain the spiritual balance we need to thread the needle.

Question One: What Are Angels?

People have all sorts of ideas concerning the identity of angels. In the movie *Michael,* John Travolta plays the part of a cigarette-smoking hang-loose slob of an angel—kind of a crude big-brother-type angel. A parapsychologist who recently appeared on an afternoon talk show identified angels as beings who do communicate with people, "But only for *noncommercial* reasons." At the funeral of the seventeen-year-old son of a former NFL star, a grieving friend was reported to have said, "He will now be my guarding angel."

People think angels are everything from the spiritual essence of departed loved ones to aliens from other worlds. While I'm certainly not a Bible scholar, I would like to rely on what it says for insight on the subject of angels.

One thing it says is that angels, like men and women, are beings created by God (Colossians 1:16). The Bible also tells us they have the ability to alter their appearance and travel instantaneously from one location to another. While they are spiritual nonmaterial beings, they do possess the ability to take on physical bodies when God sends them on a special task that requires a body. A classic example from the Bible occurred when the three angels appeared to Abraham and told him about the impending doom of Sodom and Gomorrah (Genesis 18). The angels looked like men and even carried on a conversation with Abraham. Later, two angels appeared to Lot in order to urge him to get out of the doomed cities and take his family with him. The appearance of the angels was such that the men of Sodom and Gomorrah thought they were men (Genesis 19).

Stories like that from the Bible cause me to be open to accounts like the one related by Billy Graham. In his best seller *Angels . . . God's Secret Agents,* Dr. Graham tells of the experience of Reverend John G. Paton, a pioneer missionary in the New Hebrides Islands. According to Mr. Paton, hostile natives surrounded his mission headquarters one night, intent on burning the Patons out and killing them. John Paton and his wife prayed all during that terror-filled night that God would deliver them. When daylight came they were amazed to see that, unaccountably, the attackers had left. They thanked God for delivering them.

A year later, the chief of the tribe was converted to Jesus Christ, and Mr. Paton asked the chief what had kept him and his men from burning down his house and killing them. The chief replied in surprise, "Who were all those men you had with you there?" The missionary answered, "There were no men. Just my wife and I." The chief argued that they had seen many men standing guard—hundreds of big men in shining garments with drawn swords in their hands. They seemed to circle the mission station, so that the natives were afraid to attack. Only then did Mr. Paton realize that God had sent his angels to protect them. The chief agreed that there was no other explanation. (Billy Graham, *Angels . . . God's Secret Agents,* Word Publishing, Dallas, London, Vancouver, Melbourne, 1986, pp. 3–4.)

Were there really angels protecting Reverend Paton and his family? I don't know. But I do know that angels can appear in human form, and I know there are times when they guard God's people.

An appearance of angels is different from a vision. A vision occurs when we are allowed a glimpse into the spiritual world. Make no mistake about it, God condemns those who seek such visions through the use of psychics or mediums (Deuteronomy 18:10–11). However, there are numerous examples in the Bible where God sent a vision to communicate something to a person.

While I've never seen an angel, there was a single occasion in my life when God granted me a vision of my deceased mother. After I've told the story, you'll see why.

In 1928 my grandfather on my mother's side of the family died. He lived on Manhattan Street in Rochester, New York, and ran the Manhattan Milk Company. He had horses that he used to pull the wagons to deliver the milk door to door. He drove one of the wagons himself and had other employees who drove the others. When he died, my grandmother sold the business for what was in those days a goodly sum.

At the same time my family lived in Rochester, where my father worked for Kodak. Because the city wanted to build a road where our house was located, they gave my father some money and we relocated. I don't know how much my father got for the land, but I do know that George Eastman himself persuaded my father to invest all of his money in Kodak stock. My dad then persuaded my grandmother to invest her money. They paid around ten cents a share for the stock during the Great Depression and then lived a frugal life.

Over the years my parents never touched the Kodak stock, and it increased in value. In 1968 my father died, leaving the stock to my mother. Later, when my first marriage fell apart, my mother remained loyal to my previous wife instead of to me. She was very angry with me for divorcing the mother of my three children and cut me out of her will. In 1984 she died before we could ever reconcile. The money wasn't important to me, but I grieved the alienation from my mother.

On January 1, 1987, I became a Christian. During the church service on Easter of that year I had just taken communion and bowed my head to pray. I closed my eyes and there, crystal clear, was my mother standing in front of me. She had on a beautiful black dress, held a patent-leather purse and wore a black hat with a veil. I immediately told God, "Please tell my mother I'm sorry. I didn't know. I was a young Christian back then."

In that moment my mother smiled and then became smaller and smaller until she disappeared. When I left church that day, I knew in my heart that I had reconciled with her.

That is the only vision I've ever had. I've never seen an angel or had a vision of God. I've certainly seen the hand of God directing my life and business—but I've never heard God's voice.

Was the vision actually my mother in angelic form? No, it was not. Angels are not the souls of departed people who can reappear to the living. They are messengers of God who carry out his commands. They are not all-powerful or all-knowing. In fact, they don't possess any of God's divine attributes. Yet the Bible makes it clear there are untold millions of these immensely powerful and well-organized spirit beings. As in *Touched by an Angel,* they think, feel, and display emotions.

All of this makes it clear to me that angels are real. They are not a product of our imagination. Right now they exist in a spiritual dimension that is parallel to our own. Occasionally, they step from their dimension to ours and allow people to see them.

Question Two: What Messages Do Angels Bring?

Since these messengers of God are here, it's reasonable to ask: *What are they trying to tell us?*

DON'T BE AFRAID

One of the most impressive series of angelic appearances took place before the birth of Jesus. Indeed, an important part of the Christmas story involves the angelic announcements to Joseph and Mary; Zechariah, the father of John the Baptist; and the shepherds who were in the fields tending their sheep.

In each instance the appearance of the angel was an impressive event. Take the appearance to the shepherds, for instance. We're told a group of shepherds were living in a field where they could keep watch over their sheep. I suspect these men were sitting around a fire making small talk. Nothing about the night seemed unusual until "An angel of the Lord appeared to them, and the glory of the Lord shone around them" (Luke 2:9–10). A few verses later we're told, "Suddenly a great company of the heavenly host appeared with the angel, praising God" (Luke 2:13).

I've had a few frightening experiences in my life, but nothing like that. The angels didn't appear off in the distance as a small light that slowly grew brighter. If they had done that the shepherds might have gotten used to the idea that something unusual was taking place. Or they might have run off—who knows?

The first angel stepped though a dimensional opening and "suddenly" was right there beside these men. The darkness of the night was dispelled by the glory of God that lit up that angel like the filament in a lightbulb. One moment it was dark. The next moment it was bright.

How did the shepherds respond to the presence of God's messenger? The Bible says they were "terrified." No kidding!

While I've never had an experience like that, I've had my share of frightening moments. Some of them were related to my personal safety or that of my family. Others had to do with concerns about a business deal. We all know what it's like to be overwhelmed with fear—if even for a moment.

The angel actually had a very important message to deliver to the shepherds. But first he spoke four words: "Do not be afraid" (Luke 2:10).

What's fascinating is that in each of the Christmas appearances of an angel, the initial message from God was the same—"Don't be afraid." God didn't want them to fear either his messenger or their circumstances.

Even a casual reading of the story shows the key players had good reason to be afraid. Mary was single and pregnant. Joseph's fiancée was expecting a child that wasn't his. The young couple realized they would be religiously and socially condemned. The father of John the Baptist had lost his speech. And the shepherds were in the presence of some supernatural being who filled their camp with light.

One of my recent battles with fear occurred when I wasn't sure of the outcome of the court ruling on *must carry* (whether or not cable systems would be required to carry local TV stations). God's message to me was "Don't worry about *must carry*." As I mentioned, it wasn't a voice I heard, but a knowing. Perhaps one of God's messengers actually sent me the same message those in ancient Israel received—"Don't be afraid."

One of the most touching angel stories I've heard is the one my friend Bill Perkins shared with me. Bill's sister, Beckie Sellers, fought a valiant battle against cancer for over fifteen years. In the fall of 1997 the disease had invaded her lungs, and she was failing fast. In the days before her death, Beckie drifted in and out of a coma. On several occasions she would open her eyes and ask those sitting at her side, "Can you see the angels?"

"No, we can't see the angels, Beckie."

With tears streaming down her cheeks she softly said, "I'm so sorry you can't see the angels. They're so beautiful."

Bill said it was as though his sister had one foot in heaven and one on earth. From that position she told those on earth what she was seeing in heaven. He said that occurrence helped ease his fear of death and strengthened his belief in the afterlife more than anything he had ever experienced.

That's what angels do. They're messengers of God who urge us to not be afraid. Our problem is we often fail to listen to God's messengers. And that gets us into trouble. I'm reminded of the story of the young man who was driving through a small West Texas town when a cop pulled him over. With a toothpick clutched between his teeth and his gut hanging over his gunbelt, the police officer strolled back to the man's car.

"You in a bit of a hurry, ain't you?"

"Yes, I am. But I can explain if you'll just give me a few minutes."

"Don't get smart with me, you heah?"

"But I know the chief of police," the young man stammered. "Just listen."

"You tellin' me what to do?"

"No, sir," the young man replied, realizing he probably should shut up.

"I think you is tellin' me what to do. Who you think you ah racing through our town like that? Now, get outta your car and put your hands behind your back. I think you need a little time in my jail. That'll slow you down."

A moment later the handcuffed prisoner was pushed into the back seat of the patrol car, driven into town, and thrown in jail.

A few hours later the cop entered the jailhouse, walked over to the young man's cell and grinned. Flicking his toothpick up and down in his mouth he said, "You lucky the police chief's daughter got married today—he probably be in a good mood when he comes in."

"I don't think so," the prisoner said with a smile. "I'm the man who was supposed to marry his daughter."

Sometimes, like that cop, we can get in such a hurry that we miss important information. We may tune out what God's messengers are saying to us. That's one reason why we need to be spiritually tuned in to God so we can sense the message his angels have for us.

EXPECT GREAT THINGS FROM GOD

After the angel had calmed the shepherds, he told them why they didn't need to be afraid. He informed them that he had come to bring good news about the birth of the Savior, Jesus Christ the Lord (Luke 2:11). The reason they didn't need to fear was because God has the power to transform despair into hope. He can take our most difficult situation and turn it into something good. God is in the business of turning lemons into lemonade.

The shepherds were living under the oppression of the Roman government. Their nation was powerless to resist. In the midst of that situation, the angels gave a message of joy. God was about to do something greater than they had ever imagined.

We experience fear when we think we lack the resources needed to overcome a problem. Angels are messengers of God who want us to know that from our greatest fears will come a demonstration of God's faithfulness. Instead of being afraid, we should look to God and anticipate the great thing he will soon do.

When I entered the luxury suite in Las Vegas shortly after midnight on New Year's Day in 1987, I was deeply depressed. That was the lowest point of my life. Yet that time of despair drove me to God. And it created in me a recognition that despairing people need something to help them connect with God. Out of that experience would come the birth of the twenty-four-hour TV service called *Worship*.

I wanted the Christian Network's *Worship* to create an atmosphere in homes and hotels that would comfort people with a sense of God's presence. Were there angels whispering in my ear? Not that I'm aware of. Maybe it was an angel who put the idea in my mind to look for a Gideon Bible in the hotel. I don't know. But I do know that when our life is the darkest the message of angels is that we shouldn't fear. Instead, we should expect God to do great things.

Occasionally, someone will report an angel doing something that clearly prepares someone for what God will do in the future. One story is about a boy in Scotland who fell into a well. His frightened playmates ran to the nearest house screaming for help. A moment later several men ran to the site of the well, fearful that the boy had already drowned. When they arrived they were surprised to find the child, dripping wet and sitting on a mound of grass beside the well.

"What happened?" one of the astounded men asked.

"A bonny man in white came and drew me out of the well," the boy told them.

Was that shiny figure an angel who pulled young Samuel Rutherford from the well so he could grow up to become a famous author and leader of the Church of Scotland? Maybe.

Those present at the time believed it was an angel. If so, then his rescue from that dark place was certainly God preparing young Samuel Rutherford for something great.

DO YOUR PART

The third message angels give us is that we have a role in God's plan and he wants us to do it. The angels told the shepherds, "You will find a baby wrapped in clothes, and lying in a manger" (Luke 2:12). While God's messenger told the shepherds what they would find, they had to go to Bethlehem and look for the baby. They had to check out the validity of the angel's promise.

A story is told about a father who was driving home from work when he stopped to watch his son play in a Little League baseball game. As he sat down behind the bench on the first baseline, he asked his son, "What's the score?"

"We're behind fourteen to nothing," his son shouted back.

"Really? Well, you don't look very discouraged?"

"Discouraged?" his son asked with a puzzled look. "Why should I be discouraged? We haven't been up to bat yet."

That boy wasn't discouraged because he hadn't done his part yet.

When the shepherds responded to the angels by walking to Bethlehem they discovered God's greatest gift to mankind. As we seek God's grace to help us thread the needle, we need to do our part. For PAX NET that means providing our country with television that advances family values and plants a spiritual seed in the heart of viewers.

Realizing that angels exist and miracles can happen puts us in touch with a spiritual reality—a reality that we need to be aware of if we're going to thread the needle.

THREAD THE NEEDLE

While cleaning out her husband's belongings, a widow discovered dozens of keys she couldn't identify. Were they relics from worthless projects long forgotten? Or were they claims to important treasure? How would she ever find out? After exhausting all suggestions, she encouraged the readers of a national newspaper column to take better care of important keys—disposing of worthless ones and marking those of value.

I think her advice is on target. Throughout this book I've given you some important keys. Each one is worth marking and holding on to. If you use them they'll enable you to discover how to bring balance to the business thread, spiritual thread, and values thread of your life. They'll help you experience the presence of God and they'll bring rewards to your life and business. Remember this line; it's one of my favorites: *"It's not over till you win."*

All of this brings me to a final question. It's one I ask myself every day: *"Bud, how are you doing getting your camel through the eye of the needle?"* And how do I answer? I tell myself that I've got the forelegs through the needle's eye, and part of the body. I won't know about the rest of the camel until my life is over. But if I make it, it will be through the grace of God.

If you finish this book on a weeknight, won't you join me tonight on PAX NET and watch Roma Downey, Della Reese, and John Dye on *Touched by an Angel.* You'll hear on tonight's episode the same words I leave with you: "God loves you."